CHILDREN OF POVERTY

Studies on the Effects of Single Parenthood, the Feminization of Poverty, and Homelessness

edited by

STUART BRUCHEY
University of Maine

A GARLAND SERIES

RUNNING FOR THEIR LIVES

Physical and Sexual Abuse of Runaway Adolescents

LESLEY A. WELSH
FRANCIS X. ARCHAMBAULT
MARK-DAVID JANUS
SCOTT W. BROWN

GARLAND PUBLISHING, Inc.
New York & London / 1995

Library of Congress Cataloging-in-Publication Data

Running for their lives : physical and sexual abuse of runaway adolescents / Lesley A. Welsh . . . [et al.].
    p.   cm. — (Children of poverty)
Includes bibliographical references (p.   ) and index.
ISBN 0-8153-2058-2
    1. Runaway teenagers—Crimes against—United States.
2. Homeless youth—Crimes against—United States.   3. Child
abuse—United States.   4. Abused children—United States.
5. Self-esteem in adolescence—United States.   I. Welsh,
Lesley A.   II. Series.
HV4505.R78   1995
362.7'4—dc20   95-7515
                                                        CIP

Printed on acid-free, 250-year-life paper
Manufactured in the United States of America

Contents

Acknowledgments

This research would not have taken place had it not been for the brave and generous contribution of the runaway and homeless youth of Covenant House-Toronto who volunteered to participate in this study for the benefit of others. We are also grateful for the cooperation of the staff of Covenant House-Toronto who protect and care for these teenagers.

We would like to thank Shirley Crawford for her patient and timely editing of each draft and for her encouragement about the value of the book. We would also like to thank David Mack for his expertise in computers; his help changed the word processor from an enigma to a friend. Nancy McIntyre has taught me many valuable strategies; her careful editing of this book is an example of the professional courtesies she extends to colleagues.

Tables

Figures

Running for Their Lives

I
Introduction

Historically, homeless and runaway youth have been a topic of interest. Tales of desperation chronicling the occurrence of physical and sexual abuse in the lives of runaway and homeless youth by Dickens (*Oliver*) and Hugo (*Les Miserables*) are in sharp contrast to tales of adventure from Twain (*Tom Sawyer*). Concern for the plight of the homeless has increased dramatically over the past decade. However, despite a great deal of rhetoric and many good intentions, the needs of this group still are not being met. One subset of the homeless for whom this is especially true is runaway adolescents. Estimates reveal that there are between 750,000 and 1,000,000 homeless runaways.[1] Tragically, it appears that as many as 75% of these youths may have suffered physical abuse or maltreatment at home during the year prior to running away.[2] Research has shown that abuse and maltreatment are linked to lowered self-esteem.[3] Nevertheless, there has been little research which investigated the incidence and nature of the abuse or its relationship to the self-esteem of the runaway adolescent.

RUNAWAYS

Previously, running away or leaving home before the age of 18 had been viewed as a bid for adventure and challenge. Today the ever-increasing awareness of the antecedents of the decision to leave home has dramatically changed the perception of running away from an adventure to an escape from years of physical, sexual, or emotional abuse. Throwaways is a term frequently used to describe youths who either are thrown out of the home or leave home because of extreme abuse.

Runaway youths are those children reported by their families to be away from home without parental permission for more than forty-eight hours. Statistics on runaway youth indicate that 3% of all families produce a runaway in a given year, and about 12% of American children are reported to authorities by their families as having run away by the time they are 18 years old.[4] This figure does not include the number of children who are thrown out of their homes or whose absences are not reported to authorities. The National Statistical Survey on Runaway Youth[5] estimated nearly one million runaway youths and also estimated that as many as one-half of runaway cases go unreported. Thus, if the one million reported runaways is an underestimate by one-half, there may be as many as two million children living on their own. These children are ill-equipped and unprepared to survive on their own. Tragically, experts testify that no more than one in three of these youths ever receive shelter once on the street, and no more than one in twelve is ever actually identified or cared for in any way.[6]

Running away, an event that is often preceded by years of conflict and abuse, exposes the youth to additional risks of abuse on the street. Powers and Eckenrode[7] reported that 66% of the runaways in their sample claimed they had experienced very severe violence on the street. Runaway youths have demonstrated higher rates of delinquency and antisocial behavior than youths who have not run away.[8] Edelbrock found that running away was associated with five problem behaviors: truancy, use of alcohol or drugs, delinquency, incorrigible misbehavior at home, and attempted suicide.[9] While delinquent and antisocial behaviors are associated with running away, it would be unfounded to assume that running away caused these behaviors. Yet, because there are few legitimate types of employment available for the increasing numbers of runaways, they may engage in socially illegitimate economic activities such as prostitution, robbery, the drug trade, and other forms of hustling.[10]

In a study by Edelbrock, personal adjustment of normal and disturbed youth was measured using the Child Behavior Checklist. The author found, that as a group, runaways were more likely to be from the disturbed group.[11] Other studies support the contention that runaway youth tend to exhibit poor personal adjustment.[12] Although disturbed youth are more likely to run away, it does not necessarily follow that most runaways are disturbed. Little research has been done to document the self-esteem of adolescent runaways. A study of 43 homeless runaway youths demonstrated that both runaways (78%) and throwaways (89%) believed they were persons of worth. In regard to self-satisfaction, 78% of the runaways and 73% of the throwaways were satisfied with themselves to some degree. However, 82% of the runaways and 79% of the throwaways saw themselves as failures, while 64% of the runaways and 63% of the throwaways were not proud of themselves. Finally, 69% of the runaways and 53% of the throwaways also reported feelings of uselessness.[13] The picture of the self-perceptions of these runaway youth is inconsistent; on one hand they reported positive self-worth, on the other hand they reported a lack of pride, a low level of satisfaction with themselves, and a belief that they are failures. Thus, at a pivotal time in identity formation, these youths are exposed to events that research has associated with risk for delinquent and violent activity, lowered self-esteem, and decreased measures of satisfaction and happiness.[14]

Adolescents who have run away from home and are living on their own on the streets may have a different attitude toward themselves than adolescents who remain in an abusive or difficult home environment. However, little is known about the abusive experiences of these runaway youths either at home or on the street, nor is there much information about the relationship of abuse to self-esteem in this population. The nature of abuse is complex and multi-faceted. The abuse suffered by runaways may have been physical, sexual, or both. Abuse suffered at home at the hands of relatives or other persons entrusted with their care may be perceived very differently from abuse suffered on the street at the hands of non-caretakers. The age of onset, severity, and frequency of abuse, as well as the relationship of the abuser to the abused may be important in understanding the impact of abuse. In addition, the impact of these events on self-esteem may be different for males and females.[15]

THEORETICAL FRAMEWORK

Multiple Risk Theory

Much of the literature deals with the causes of abuse. However, several theoretical frameworks support hypotheses concerning the consequences of abuse. Some children who experience abuse suffer life-long consequences, while other children are resilient in the face of abuse. Multiple risk theory suggests that long-term negative consequences are more likely to occur when there is an accumulation of risk factors in the child's environment. The risk of developmental harm from violence and abuse increases when other risk factors such as poor parental relations, poverty, and lack of social support are present.[16] Age of onset of abuse, severity, frequency, and identity of perpetrator of the abuse may represent variations in the accumulated risk factors that predict negative outcomes such as negative self-esteem. Risk theory would also suggest that the decision to run away may be affected by the accumulation risk factors and the absence of support factors.

Interpersonal Violence Literature

The interpersonal violence literature has documented the negative effect of both physical and sexual abuse on the self-esteem of the victim.[17] While most runaways exhibit a long history of abuse, there is some research that indicates a single episode of abuse may result in the same behavioral and emotional consequences as multiple episodes.[18] Perhaps the quality of the parent-child relationship may be as predictive of negative behavioral and emotional adjustment as the number and nature of the abusive events. Erickson, Egeland, and Pianta[19] suggest that abusive behavior typically takes place within a pervasive, persistent pattern of dysfunctional family interactions. This pattern of interaction, rather than the abuse by itself, may account for the psychological outcomes of the child.

Self-Esteem Theory

Self-esteem. Self-esteem is a global sense of self-worth. It is that dimension of the self-concept that involves the worth or value one places on oneself. It is an attitude towards the self and, as such, it takes on either a positive or negative valence. It is a general measure of self-worth, also referred to as self-acceptance.[20]

In contrast to self-esteem, Byrne and Shavelson hypothesize that self-concept is both multidimensional and hierarchical. Their model places perceptions of behavior at the base, moving to inferences about self in specific areas (e.g., mathematics), then to inferences about self in broader areas (e.g., academic), and finally, to inferences about self in general. Self-esteem is this last, overarching, generalized perception of self.[21]

Correlates of Self-Esteem. The far-reaching influence of self-esteem is reflected in the literature. Studies abound linking self-esteem to major social, emotional, and behavioral variables. Social interactions begin in infancy and continue throughout life. Thus, patterns that began in infancy may still be influencing our behaviors and reactions to our environment. Interestingly, the quality of parents' interactions with their children often may be related to the quality of their own parents' interactions with them during their childhood. There is evidence that adults who were abused or maltreated as children have an increased likelihood of abusing or maltreating their own children.[22]

Parenting styles are frequently associated with parental level of self-esteem. In a study of 74 mothers (18 abusive, 19 neglecting, and 37 control), the abusive mothers were found to have lower self-esteem than the neglecting or control mothers.[23] Steele and Pollock found both abusive and neglecting mothers to have low self-esteem.[24] Parental traits are also related to the self-esteem of the child during adolescence.[25] Low self-esteem has been associated with both the abuser and the abused. Thus, self-esteem effects can be traced starting with parents and continuing through their offspring.

Self-esteem has been associated with psychological health. Emotional well-being often has been associated with high self-esteem, while emotional problems have been associated with low esteem. Individual reactions to adversity vary; some people are able to adapt and cope, while others become clinically depressed. There is some indication that the difference in response between individuals can, in part, be attributed to self-esteem.[26]

The importance of self-concept, of which self-esteem is a dimension, in academic achievement has been debated in the literature. A meta-analysis by Song and Hattie uncovered diverse findings, from which it has been hypothesized that self-concept exerts an indirect effect on academic achievement. However, academic progress is associated with level of self-esteem.[27] Thus, the development of a positive self-esteem can have far-reaching influence. It has been associated with important psychological, educational, and interpersonal behaviors.

Another powerful influence on self-esteem is our own evaluation of personal performance. We form judgments concerning our own performances and, if these performances fall short of our expectations, our self-esteem suffers. On the other hand, when we meet or exceed personal expectations, our self-esteem is enhanced. While our self-perceptions are influencing our behavior, the outcomes of our interactions are influencing our self-perceptions. This two-way influence is called reciprocal determinism. Reciprocal determinism is a component of social cognitive theory which views self-esteem as both caused by and causing the behaviors individuals choose when interacting with their environment.

Social Cognitive Theory

Social learning theory, more recently called social cognitive theory (SCT), provides an additional framework for this study. Self-esteem, a component of self-concept, is a complex set of inter-related thoughts and judgments concerning one's own self. Social cognitive theory holds self-concept as a central motivating force in behavior.[28] For example, individuals with high self-esteem will expect positive interactions with their environment, and this expectation of success will influence their behavior. Research has demonstrated that individuals with high expectations of success engage in more activities, persist at tasks longer, and derive more satisfaction from the tasks. On the other hand, individuals with low self-esteem will have lower expectations of success and may derive less satisfaction and avoid the activity. Thus, personal perceptions of self influence all social interactions and behaviors. Whereas, self-esteem has been identified as an important variable in the study of adolescents, there is virtually no literature on the self-esteem of adolescents who have run away.

Although self-esteem is influenced by social comparisons, reflected appraisals, and self appraisal of personal performance, it is important to recognize that the immediate environment or context may have a stronger influence than that of the larger, more distant, society. In a large scale study of 5,024 high school juniors and seniors, Rosenberg examined the self-esteem of both Black and White students.[29] The Black students were expected to exhibit lower self-esteem than the White students because they had been subjected historically to prejudice and discrimination and, typically, had lower educational and occupational success. However, results from the 1965 study found either weak or negative correlations between ethnicity and self-esteem, with the Black students exhibiting higher self-esteem than the White students.

Rosenberg explains how these unexpected results correspond to the self-esteem perspective.[30] It had been assumed that the reflected appraisals of the Black population by the broader society would damage their self-esteem, but rather it was the reflected appraisal of significant others that had the greatest impact on self-esteem. Thus, an adolescent is able to maintain high self-regard if the immediate environment is supportive and reflective of high regard, regardless of the appraisals of a distant and non-interactive larger society. The most powerful impact on self-esteem comes from the opinion of those with whom one interacts directly and frequently. Likewise, people with whom one interacts directly and frequently are used as a comparison or standard by which one judges oneself. Therefore, both reflected appraisals and social comparisons must be examined in the context of the immediate environment. The decision to run away dramatically alters the immediate environment. After leaving an abusive or dysfunctional home, the people with whom the runaway interacts daily may hold very different opinions and provide strikingly different standards of comparison than those encountered in the home. Therefore the act of running away may precipitate a change in self-esteem.

Adolescence

Adolescence. Adolescence, as a distinct developmental stage in the human life cycle, is a relatively recent concept. Traditionally, puberty hails the onset of adolescence, while economic independence marks the entry into adulthood. Two events have caused the period of adolescence to be extended from a relatively short period in pre-industrial times to nearly a decade in modern times. First, puberty now occurs three to four years earlier, at about 11 or 12 years of age. Second, the necessity for prolonged education in a technological society has lengthened the time before entry into adulthood. Thus, adolescence spans a period of about 10 years during which the youth ideally prepares for life, a time for the training and education that provides options for the individual's future.[31]

Until recently, adolescence has often been considered a period of development when "storm and stress" were considered the norm.[32] Today this perception has been replaced by a view of adolescence as a time of change, characterized by good relationships with parents and increasing self-reliance and autonomy.[33] Adolescents must cope with change in many areas of their lives. These youngsters must adjust to their rapidly changing bodies, and changing roles within the family and school, while acquiring increasing independence and making occupational decisions. These changes, while substantial, are not necessarily accompanied by disruption or crisis, but rather by coping and development.[34]

In light of changing roles and expectations, it is no wonder that self-esteem development is critical during this period of heightened awareness of self and of increased ability to form self-evaluations.[35] The need to establish a personal identity coupled with increasing cognitive abilities lend validity to the claim that adolescence is a time when identity formation occurs.[36]

The development of positive self-esteem in adolescents has been linked to the quality of interpersonal relationships. Of particular importance is the quality of the parent-child relationship with parental support, encouragement, and affection predictive of positive self-esteem in both male and female adolescents. The importance of peer relationships is greater for females than for males, while male self-esteem is more performance-based.[37] Thus, adolescence is a time characterized by physiological, cognitive, and identity development. It is a time between childhood and adulthood during which the youth prepares for the assumption of adult roles.[38] Running away typically disrupts education and prematurely thrusts the youth into the role of sole provider. A role that the youth is ill-prepared to undertake. Early literature that portrayed running away as an adventure-seeking experience has given way to a realization that a high proportion of runaways have lived in abusive home environments for much of their lives. Farber and Joseph concludes that physical abuse contributed to the cause and continuance of the runaway episode.[39]

Most of the previous research has been conducted within the family context and generalized to runaways. This book presents the results of a study that examines each of these variables in a population of runaway adolescents.

The purpose of this book is to describe:
- previous research on physical abuse in the general and runaway population,
- previous research on sexual abuse in the general population,
- the adolescents who participated in this study and their circumstances and reasons for running away,
- the nature and incidence of the physical abuse suffered by these adolescents at home and on the street,
- the nature, incidence, and perpetrators of the sexual abuse experienced by these adolescents, and

- a model of the inter-relationships among self-esteem of runaway adolescents and physical and sexual abuse factors, such as age of onset, frequency and severity.

The plight of homeless youth is of immediate concern. Policy decisions regarding the care and treatment of these children need to be guided by both detailed and accurate information. Effective intervention is necessary to break the cycle of abuse and neglect. Self-esteem has been identified as an important variable in intervention and education programs. Understanding the incidence and nature of physical and sexual abuse of adolescent runaways will be of major importance to policy makers, care providers, and educators of these youth. The challenge of providing runaway youth with the skills and resources necessary to become productive citizens is imposing. Knowledge of the trends and patterns in the histories, experiences, and self-esteem of runaway youth will greatly enhance the probability of successfully meeting this challenge.

NOTES

1. Garbarino, J., & Gilliam, G. (1980). *Understanding abusive families.* Lexington, MA: Lexington Books.
2. Farber, E., & Egeland, B. (1987). Invulnerability among abused and neglected children. In E.J. Anthony & B. Cohler (Eds.), *The invulnerable child* (pp. 253-288). New York: Guiford Press.
3. Schneider-Rosen, K, & Cicchetti, D. (1984). The relationship between affect and cognition in maltreated infants: Quality of attachment and the development of visual self-recognition. *Child Development,* 55, 648-658.
4. Garbarino, J., Wilson, J., & Garbarino, A. (1986). The adolescent runaway. In J. Garbarino, C. Schellenbach, & J. Sebes (Eds.), *Troubled youth, troubled families.* New York: Aldine Publishing.
5. Opinion Research Corporation. (1976). *National statistical survey of runaway youth.* Princeton, NJ: Opinion Research Corp.
6. House Committee on Education and Labor, Subcommittee of Human Resources. (1984). *Juvenile Justice, Runaway youth and missing children's act,* Amendments, 98th Congress, 2nd Session, 7 March.

7. Powers, J., & Eckenrode, J. (1988). The maltreatment of adolescents. *Child Abuse and Neglect*, 12(2), 189-200.

8. Goldberg, M. (1972). Runaway Americans. *Mental Hygiene*, 56, 13-21.

9. Edelbrock, C. (1980). Running away from home: Incidence and correlates among children and youth referred for mental health services. *Journal of Family Issues*, 1(2), 210-228.

10. Garbarino, J., Wilson, J., & Garbarino, A. (1986). The adolescent runaway. In J. Garbarino, C. Schellenbach, & J. Sebes (Eds.), *Troubled youth, troubled families*. New York: Aldine.

11. Edelbrock, C. (1980). Running away from home: Incidence and correlates among children and youth referred for mental health services. *Journal of Family Issues*, 1(2), 210-228.

12. Jenkins, R.L., & Boyer, A. (1968). Types of delinquent behavior and background factors. *International Journal of Social Psychiatry*, 14, 65-75.

13. Adams, G.R., Gullotla, T., & Clancy, M.A. (1985). Homeless adolescents: A descriptive study of similarities and differences between runaways and throwaways. *Adolescence*, 20(79), 715-724.

14. Janus, M.D., McCormack, A., Burgess, A.W., & Hartman, C. (1987). *Adolescent runaways: Causes and consequences.* Lexington, MA: Lexington Books.

15. Ibid.

16. Garbarino, J., Dubrow, N., Kostelny, K. & Pardo, C. (1992). *Children in danger: Coping with the consequences of community violence*. San Francisco: Jossey-Bass.

17. Schneider-Rosen, K, & Cicchetti, D. (1984). The relationship between affect and cognition in maltreated infants: Quality of attachment and the development of visual self-recognition. *Child Development*, 55, 648-658.

18. Farber, E., & Joseph, J. (1985). The maltreated adolescent: Patterns of physical abuse. *Child Abuse and Neglect*, 9(2), 201-206.

19. Erickson, M.F., Egeland, B., & Pianta, R. (1989). The effects of maltreatment on the development of young children. In D. Cicchetti & V. Carlson (Eds.), *Child maltreatment: Theory and research on the causes and consequences of child abuse and neglect* (pp. 647-684). New York: Cambridge University Press.

20. Rosenberg, M. (1989). *Society and the adolescent self-image*. Middletown, CT: Wesleyan University Press.

21. Byrne, B.M., & Shavelson, R.J. (1986). On the structure of adolescent self-concept. *Journal of Educational Psychology*, 78, 474-481.

22. Pianta, R., Egeland, B., & Erickson, M.E. (1989). The antecedents of maltreatment: Results of the mother-child interaction research project. In D. Cicchetti & V. Carlson (Eds.), *Child maltreatment: Theory and research on the causes and consequences of child abuse and neglect* (pp. 203-253). New York: Cambridge University Press.

23. Culp, R.E., Culp, A.M. 1989). Self-esteem and depression in abusive, neglecting, and nonmaltreating mothers. *Infant Mental Health Journal*, 10(4), 243-251.

24. Steele, B.F., & Pollock, C.B. (1974). Psychiatric study of abusive parents. In R.E. Helfer & C.H. Kempe (Eds.), *The battered child*. Chicago: University of Chicago Press.

25. Hill, J.P., & Holbeck, G.N. (1986). Attachment and autonomy during adolescence. In I.G. Whitehurst (Ed.), *Annals of child development*: Vol. I (pp. 145-189). Greenwich, CT: JAI.

26. Culp, R.E., Culp, A.M. 1989). Self-esteem and depression in abusive, neglecting, and nonmaltreating mothers. *Infant Mental Health Journal*, 10(4), 243-251.

27. Song, I.S., & Hattie, J. (1984). Home environment, self-concept, and academic achievement: A causal modeling approach. *Journal of Educational Psychology*, 76(6), 1269-1281.

28. Bandura, A. (1986). *Social foundation of thought and action: A social cognitive theory*. Englewood Cliffs, NJ: Prentice Hall.

29. Rosenberg, M. (1965). *Society and adolescent self-image*. Princeton, NJ: Princeton University Press.

30. Rosenberg, M. (1989). *Society and the adolescent self-image*. Middletown, CT: Wesleyan University Press.

31. Muuss, R.E. (1990). *Adolescent behavior and society*. New York: McGraw-Hill Publishing Co.

32. Hall, G.S. (1904). *Adolescence* (Vols. I & II). Englewood Cliffs, NJ: Prentice Hall.

33. Muuss, R.E. (1990). *Adolescent behavior and society*. New York: McGraw-Hill Publishing Co.

34. Steinberg, L. (1987). The impact of puberty on family relations: Effects of pubertal status and pubertal timing. *Developmental Psychology*, 23, 451-460.

35. Piaget, J. (1952). *The origins of intelligence in children.* New York: International Press.

36. Erikson, E.H. (1968). *Identity: youth and crisis.* New York: Norton.

37. Walker, L.S., & Green, J.W. (1986). The social context of adolescent self-esteem. *Journal of Youth and Adolescence*, 15(4), 315-322.

38. Hamburg, D.A. (1986). Preparing for life: The critical transition of adolescence. (Annual report of the President). New York: Carnegie Corp.

39. Farber, E., & Joseph, J. (1985). The maltreated adolescent: Patterns of physical abuse. *Child Abuse and Neglect*, 9(2), 201-206.

II
Physical Abuse of Children and Adolescents

The view of the family as a place of safety and security is belied by the growing awareness that the chance of experiencing violence in the home may be greater than on the streets.[1] However, one major obstacle confronting researchers in the field of family and interpersonal violence is the lack of consistent definitions of abuse. Statistics concerning incidence and prevalence are plagued by inconsistencies. Some authors include any physical act as an indication of abuse, such as slapping or spanking, while other authors only include extreme physical acts that result in physical injury.

In spite of these difficulties, it is clear that domestic violence exists in all sectors of society.[2] According to FBI statistics, nearly 20% of all murders are committed between family members, and almost one third of all female homicide victims are killed by their husbands or boyfriends. A random survey of women living in San Francisco indicated that 2.5% had been coerced before they were 18 years old into oral, anal, or genital intercourse by their father, stepfather, or brother.[3] In 1982, although there were nearly one million official reports of child abuse or neglect, researchers felt that official reports underestimated true incidence. There are indications of differential rates of reporting suspected child abuse among socioeconomic (SES) levels, with high and medium SES somewhat insulated from official reports. Therefore, official estimates of abuse must be considered an underestimate of the true incidence.

PHYSICAL ABUSE

Before presenting physical abuse rates of runaway adolescents, the incidence of physical abuse in the general population will be discussed. Incidence is defined as the rate per one thousand

15

cases; thus an incidence of 5 means an occurance in 5 cases out of a thousand. On the other hand, percent is reported as rate out of a hundred cases. An incidence of 5 would be equivalent to .5%. Several studies examine the incidence of officially reported cases of abuse; however, official reports of child abuse include a number of biases. Certain individuals and families are more likely to be reported due to the nature of the injury, social status of the alleged abused, and social characteristics of the victim. Minority, poor, and single parents are more likely to be correctly and incorrectly reported as abusers than are white, wealthy, and intact family members. Infants are more likely to be identified as victims than teenagers.[4] It is estimated that approximately one-half of the incidents of physical abuse remain unreported.

Despite the limitations of official reporting, the collected statistics shed light on the phenomenon. The 1981 National Incidence Study conducted by the National Center for Child Abuse and Neglect estimated a rate of physical abuse of 3.4 per thousand.[5] A report by the American Association for Protecting Children reported a physical abuse rate of 6.8 per thousand.[6] Much of the variation in the rates of reported abuse can be explained by differing definitions of abuse used by reporting agencies. This exemplifies why the development of consistent behavioral definitions of abuse is critical to the advancement of knowledge in the field.

In landmark studies of family violence, the Family Violence Survey of 1975 and the Family Resurvey of 1985 gathered domestic violence information from a representative sample of subjects.[7] The original survey comprised more than 2,000 households consisting of a couple and at least one child between the ages of three and seventeen. The participants were asked to describe ways in which they resolved conflicts within the family during the last year. This sample had major advantages over the use of clinical samples or official reports. Official reports and clinical samples represent extreme cases, while the Family Violence Surveys represent the general population. Another advantage of the Family Violence Surveys is the behavioral categorization of the severity of violence and abuse (see Figure 1). Minor Violence acts are defined as throwing something at, pushing, grabbing, shoving,

Figure 1
Definitions of Categories of Violence[8]

Categories of Violence

A. Minor Violence Acts
   1. Threw something
   2. Pushed/grabbed/shoved
   3. Slapped or spanked

B. Very Severe Violence Acts*
   4. Kicked/bit/hit with fist
   5. Beat up
   6. Threatened with or used gun or weapon
   7. Choked
   8. Burned
   9. Scalded

---

* Defined as abuse.

Note. A third category, Severe Violence, including all the Very Severe Violence acts plus hitting or attempting to hit with an object proved too controversial to be defined as abuse.

slapping, or spanking. These acts while physically punitive in nature are not defined as abusive. Minor Violence acts are behaviors that are accepted by many people as normal disciplinary actions. Very Severe Violence acts include kicking, biting, hitting with a fist, beating up, choking, burning, scalding, or using a gun or knife. Any act from the Very Severe Violence category is defined as abusive. Therefore, in this study, Minor Violence acts are defined as traditional physical punishment, while Very Severe Violence acts are defined as abusive assaults. A third category Severe Violence includes all the Very Severe acts plus hitting with an object. Hitting with an object proved to be too imprecise to be useful, because the object could range from a strap which could be considered a normal disciplinary act to a frying pan which would be clearly abusive. Therefore Severe Violence is not defined as abuse. Although these definitions may be controversial, they are clearly defined by specific behaviors providing a basis for interpretation, compilation, and comparison of the results.

Although The Family Violence Survey of 1975 had several advantages over studies consisting of officially reported cases in establishing the prevalence of abuse in American households, limiting the sample to two-parent households was a disadvantage. Research suggests a link between single parents and the increased risk of abuse.[9] Additionally, much abuse occurs to children under three years of age who were not included in the survey's sample.[10] Both of these limitations would indicate that the incidence rates reported in The Family Violence Survey may be low. In the 1975 study, the incidence of young victims experiencing Very Severe forms of violence (abuse) is 36 per thousand. At this conservative estimate, 1.5 million children were reported to have experienced Severe forms of physical abuse in 1975.

The Family Violence Resurvey of 1985 included single parents and families with children under 3 years old. However, when comparisons are made to the rates of violence in 1975 the researchers use three reporting methods: (1) a subset of subjects that is consistent with the 1975 sample (two-parent households with children between 3 and 17), (2) the subset including single parents and children between 0 and 17 , and (3) the subset including single parents and children between 15 and 17. Table 1 shows comparisons among rates of violence for the different samples. The 1985 survey showed a decline in the incidence of abuse (Severe Violence) from 36 per thousand (1 out of 28 children) to 19 per thousand (1 out of 53 children) when a comparable subset was studied. Interestingly the number of officially reported cases of child maltreatment showed a 225% increase from 1976 to 1987.[11] This may reflect a growing awareness of the seriousness of child abuse which would explain the decrease in the incidence reported within families as well as the increased rate of reporting suspected abuse.

Comparisons of the three sets of data from the 1985 Survey (See Table 1) yields some information about the patterns of violence within families. When children under the age of 3 are included, virtually 100% of the youth in the United States experienced some form of physical force within the last year. These data suggest that milder forms of violence are more common with younger children, while adolescents experience more severe forms of violence within their families.

Table 1
Rate per Thousand of Violence Across Time[12]

Violence Categories	1975	1985[a]	1985[b]	1985[c]
Very severe (Abuse)	36	19	23	21
Severe violence	140	107	110	70
Any violence	630	620	999	340

a. Two parents and children between 3 - 17. b. Including single parents and children between 0 - 17. c. Including single parent and children between 15 - 17.

Age of Onset

Cases of officially reported physical abuse suggest that onset of abuse may occur at a very early age for many children. Research indicates that very young children (three months to five years) are at the highest risk of abuse.[13] Several studies have found that, while very young children are at risk, the risk again increases during adolescence.[14]

The National Incidence Study found that 47% of all officially reported child abuse cases involved adolescents.[15] However, the National Family Violence Survey suggests that the frequency of less severe violent acts is highest in the very young child and that the frequency of the most severe violent acts is unrelated to age.[16]

Gender

Most studies report males to be at higher risk of physical abuse than females.[17] A pattern appears to emerge; males are at greatest risk below the age of 12, while females become the more likely victim during adolescence.[18] This pattern may reflect males' increase in strength and the ability to protect themselves as they mature. This trend may be due to an actual decrease in violent behavior towards male adolescents or to a perceived decrease in adolescent male vulnerability and a subsequent decrease in defining violent acts to adolescent males as abuse.[19]

Perpetrator

Research indicates that mothers are the most frequent perpetrators of physical abuse.[20] Mothers are the primary caretakers, and as such, spend more time interacting with the child. This may explain the increased frequency of abuse by mothers. However, studies have found that fathers cause more abusive injuries than mothers.[21] Therefore, while the actual number of abusive incidents may be higher for mothers these incidents are not likely to be severe enough to cause injury. On the other hand, while the actual number of abusive incidents may be lower for fathers, the likelihood is greater that the abuse will be severe enough to cause an injury.

Severity

The Family Violence Resurvey of 1985 showed that the severity of violence is related to the age of the child. The rate of Minor Violence to children between three and six years is 89%; in adolescence this rate declines to 29%. This trend is seen also in the rate of Severe Violence. Although Straus and Gelles did not find a relationship between age and Very Severe Violence, Rosenthal found a significant relationship between increased severity of abuse and younger age. Thus, age appears to be related to both minor and severe violence, but not related to very severe violence.

Gender has also been shown to be a factor in severity of abuse. Male victims were reported to have a higher incidence of both severe injuries and fatalities.[22]

Frequency

Violence that occurs infrequently may have a different effect than violence that occurs daily. Additionally, the long-term effect of one period of violence may differ from chronic violence over the course of a lifetime. Very few studies examine this aspect of violence. Several studies indicate that patterns of violence or non-violence seem to remain relatively constant.[23]

The frequency of attack seems to be related to the severity of the attack. Straus and Gelles reported Minor Violence occurred with less frequency (eight times a year) than Very Severe Violence acts (17 times a year).[24] In 1986 Straus reported that as the frequency of normative physical punishment increased, so did the score on the Child Abuse Checklist. This indicates that frequent use of physical punishment may increase the likelihood of abusive behaviors.[25]

Effects of Physical Abuse

The psychological and behavioral consequences of child abuse are important concerns. Straus and Gelles reported that child abuse victims had two to three times higher rates of problem behaviors, such as temper tantrums, failing grades in school, disciplinary problems in school and at home, physically assaultive behavior at home and outside the home, vandalism and theft, and alcohol and drug use.[26] Overall 21% of abused women reported feeling worthless. These feelings of worthlessness were related to the severity of the abuse. Also, maltreated children have demonstrated multiple forms of socially dysfunctional behaviors: aggression[27], withdrawal or passivity[28], and inability to make friends.[29] Martin concluded, after a comprehensive review of the existing literature on the effects of maltreatment, that psychological problems are a major form of harm that can result from abuse and neglect.[30] Oates contended that the effects of abuse and neglect outlive the immediate traumatic situation and may handicap the child throughout his or her life.[31] Lack of trust and low self-esteem are recurring themes in the lives of survivors of childhood abuse.

Some researchers contend that it may be the dysfunctional family environment, rather that the physical abuse, that is predictive of the negative consequences. Egeland and Sroufe found, in a longitudinal study, that physically abused children differed from verbally abused children in several ways: increased anger, frustration, noncompliance, whining, negative affect, and less positive affect.[32] On the other hand, the children suffering from the lowest self-esteem were the neglected, but not physically abused, group. Attention, even in the form of abuse, appears to result in less damaging consequences than neglect.[33] Abused and non-abused siblings were found to exhibit similar personal adjustment characteristics.[34] Thus, some evidence indicates that the family characteristics that tolerate child abuse may produce similar psychological and behavioral disturbances in both abused and non-abused children.

At present, it is not possible to predict the specific effects of physical abuse; however, several themes do emerge from this research. First, reactions to abuse demonstrate considerable variation; some victims exhibit no obvious long-term effects, while others demonstrate a variety of consequences ranging from low self-esteem to aggression. Second, the presence or absence of abuse appears to interact with other aspects of the child's environment to determine consequences. Lynch and Roberts concluded that a dysfunctional family environment may be a larger factor in determining self-esteem than the abuse per se. Some important factors associated with effect of abuse are degree of maternal involvement, age at onset of abuse, severity and frequency of abuse, as well as family stress and overall family dynamics. Cicchetti hypothesized that even resilient children, who exhibit no immediately observable negative consequences of abuse, may manifest vulnerability at a later developmental period.[35] However, Farber and Egeland concluded that very few abused children appear invulnerable to the negative effects of abuse.[36]

Physical Abuse of Runaways

Documentation of parental maltreatment as a major factor in running away is mounting. For youths who are exposed to chronic mistreatment at the hands of parents or caretakers, running away from home may be viewed as a healthy and adaptive response to a negative situation.[37] Houghten and Golembiewski concluded that more than 80% of all serious runaway episodes involve maltreatment.[38] Farber and his associates found that 75% of runaway youth report being victims of severe maltreatment the year prior to running.[39] Families of runaway youth have demonstrated patterns of poor conflict resolution, inadequate communication, and ineffective parental supervision.[40] Parental maltreatment is increasingly recognized as a causal element in running away.[41]

The consequences of running away, such as involvement in crime or repeated victimization, appear to be the most severe for those youth who have already experienced victimization at home prior to running away.[42] Thus, within a group who have been identified with a high rate of delinquent and antisocial behaviors and increasingly identified with high rates of familial abuse and neglect, there is evidence that the experience of abuse may be a more important predictor of delinquent behavior than the actual runaway incident.

NOTES

1. Gelles, R.J., & Cornell, C.P. (1990). *Intimate violence in families.* Newbury Park, CA: Sage Publications, Inc.

2. Cicchetti, D., & Carlson, V. (1989). *Child maltreatment: Theory and research on the causes and consequences of child abuse and neglect.* Cambridge, MA: Cambridge University Press.

3. Russell, D.E. (1986). *The secret trauma: Incest in the lives of girls and women.* New York: Basic Books.

4. Hampton, R., & Newberger, E.H. (1988). Child abuse incidence and reporting by hospitals: The significance of severity, class, and race. *American Journal of Public Health,* 75, 56-69.

5. National Center on Child Abuse and Neglect (NCCAN). (1981). Study findings: *National study of incidence and severity of child abuse and neglect.* Washington, DC: Department of Health, Education, and Welfare.

6. American Association for Protecting Children. (1986). *Highlights of official child neglect and abuse reporting,* 1984. Denver: American Humane Association.

7. Straus, M., & Gelles, R. (1986). Societal change and change in family violence from 1975-1985 as revealed by two national surveys. *Journal of Marriage and the Family,* 48, 465-489.

8. Straus, M. Gelles, R., & Steinmetz, S. (1981). *Behind closed doors: Violence in the American family.* Newbury Park, CA: Sage Publications Inc.

9. Straus, M., & Gelles, R. (1988). How violent are American families. In G. Hotaling, D. Finkelhor, J. Kirkpatrick, & M. Straus (Eds.), *Family abuse and its consequences: New directors in research.* Beverly Hills, CA: Sage Publications.

10. Straus, M., & Gelles, R. (1988). How violent are American families. In G. Hotaling, D. Finkelhor, J. Kirkpatrick, & M. Straus (Eds.), *Family abuse and its consequences: New directors in research.* Beverly Hills, CA: Sage Publications.

11. American Association for Protecting Children. (1989). *Highlights of official child neglect and abuse reporting, 1987.* Denver: American Humane Association.

12. Straus, M. Gelles, R., & Steinmetz, S. (1981). *Behind closed doors: Violence in the American family.* Newbury Park, CA.: Sage Publications Inc.

13. Gelles, R.J. (1987). *The violent home.* Newbury Park, CA: Sage Publications, Inc.

14. Garbarino, Schellenbach, Sebes, & Associates. (1986). *Troubled youth, troubled families.* New York: Aldine Publishing.

15. Powers, J., & Eckenrode, J. (1988). The maltreatment of adolescents. *Child Abuse and Neglect*, 12(2), 189-200.

16. Straus, M., & Gelles, R. (1989). *Physical violence in American families*. New Brunswick, NJ: Transaction Publishers.

17. American Association for Protecting Children. (1986). *Highlights of official child neglect and abuse reporting, 1984*. Denver: American Humane Association.

18. Olsen, L., & Holmes, W. (1983). *Youth at risk: Adolescents and maltreatment*. Boston, MA: Center for Applied Social Research.

19. Powers, J., & Eckenrode, J. (1988). The maltreatment of adolescents. *Child Abuse and Neglect*, 12(2), 189-200.

20. American Association for Protecting Children. (1986). *Highlights of official child neglect and abuse reporting, 1984*. Denver: American Humane Association.

21. Bryan, J.W., & Freed, F.W. (1982). Corporal punishment: Normative data and sociological and psychological correlates in a community college population. *Journal of Youth and Adolescence*, 11, 77-82.

22. American Association for Protecting Children. (1986). *Highlights of official child neglect and abuse reporting, 1984*. Denver: American Humane Association.

23. Herrenkohl, R.C., Herrenkohl, E.C., Egolf, B., & Seech, M. (1980). The repetition of child abuse: How frequently does it occur? In *The abused child in the family and in the community: Selected papers from the second International Congress on Child Abuse and Neglect*, London, 1978, Vol. 1, edited by C.H. Kempe, A.W. Franklin, & C. Cooper. Oxford: Pergamon Press.

24. Straus, M., & Gelles, R. (1989). *Physical violence in American families*. New Brunswick, NJ: Transaction Publishers.

25. Straus, M., & Gelles, R. (1986). Societal change and change in family violence from 1975-1985 as revealed by two national surveys. *Journal of Marriage and the Family*, 48, 465-489.

26. Straus, M., & Gelles, R. (1989). *Physical violence in American families*. New Brunswick, NJ: Transaction Publishers.

27. Herrenkohl, R.C., & Herrenkohl, E.C. (1981). Some antecedents and developmental consequences of child maltreatment. In R. Rizley & D. Cicchetti (Eds.), *Developmental perspectives on child maltreatment*. San Francisco: Jossey-Bass.

28. Crittenden, P.M. (1981). Abusing, neglecting, problematic, and adequate dyads: Differentiating by patterns of interaction. *Merrill-Palmer Quarterly*, 27, 201-208.

29. Reidy, T.J. (1977). The aggressive characteristics of abused and neglected children. *Journal of Clinical Psychology*, 33, 1140-1145.

30. Martin, H.P. (1980). The consequences of being abused and neglected: How the child fares. In C.H. Kempe & R.E. Helfer (Eds.), *The battered child (3rd ed.)*. Chicago: University of Chicago Press.

31. Oates, K. (1986). *Child abuse and neglect: What happens eventually?* New York: Brunner/Mazel.

32. Egeland, B., & Sroufe, L.A. (1981). Development sequelae of maltreatment in infancy. *New Directions of Child Development: Developmental Perspectives in Child Maltreatment*, 11, 77-92.

33. Egeland, B., Sroufe, L.A., & Erickson, M.F. (1983). Developmental consequences of different patterns of maltreatment. *Child Abuse and Neglect*, 7(4), 459-469.

34. Lynch, M.A., & Roberts, J. (1977). Predicting child abuse: Signs of bonding failure in the maternity hospital. *British Medical Journal*, 1, 624-626.

35. Cicchetti, D. (1989). How research on child maltreatment has informed the study of child development: Perspectives from developmental psychology. In D. Cicchetti & V. Carlson (Eds.), *Child maltreatment* (pp. 377-432). New York: Cambridge University Press.

36. Farber, E., & Egeland, B. (1987). Invulnerability among abused and neglected children. In E.J. Anthony & B. Cohler (Eds.), *The invulnerable child* (pp. 253-288). New York: Guilford Press.

37. Silbert, M.H., & Pines, A.M. (1981). Sexual child abuse as an antecedent to prostitution. *Child Abuse and Neglect*, 5, 407-411.

38. Houghten, T., & Golembiewski, M. (1976). *A study of runaway youth and their families*. Washington, DC: Youth Alternatives Project.

39. Farber, E., Kinast, C., McCoard, W., & Falkner, D. (1984). Violence in families of adolescent runaways. *Child Abuse and Neglect*, 8(3), 295-299.

40. Garbarino, Schellenbach, Sebes, & Associates. (1986). *Troubled youth, troubled families*. New York: Aldine Publishing.

41. Liebertoff, K. (1980). The runaway child in America. *Journal of Family Issues*, 1, 151-164.

42. Garbarino, J., Wilson, J., & Garbarino, A. (1986). The adolescent runaway. In J. Garbarino, C. Schellenbach, & J. Sebes (Eds.), *Troubled youth, troubled families.* New York: Aldine Publishing.

III
Sexual Abuse of Children and Adolescents

Sexual exploitation is a term that includes rape, child sexual abuse, and sexual harassment.[1] Child sexual abuse may be defined as contacts and interactions between a child and an adult when the child is being used for the sexual stimulation of the perpetrator or another person. Sexual interaction between children when one child is substantially older or more powerful is also considered abusive.[2] Child sexual abuse may or may not involve the use of force, but usually involves the violation of trust, power, and authority.

SEXUAL ABUSE

The research concerning sexual abuse suffers from many of the same limitations as the physical abuse literature: (a) lack of a consistent or behaviorally-based definition of sexual abuse, (b) differing policies and procedures for the compiling and reporting of officially reported sexual abuse, (c) biases in the reporting of abuse particularly with respect of socioeconomic levels, and (d) the reliance on officially reported cases, clinical samples, and studies of adults' recollection abuse in their childhood. The estimates of the prevalence of child abuse show a great deal of variation; much of this variation can be explained by the limitations listed previously.

Legal Sanctions

Most states have legal sanctions against sexual activity between children and older persons. However, there is a great deal of variation in the statutes. In most states the age of sexual consent is 16; however in some states it is as low as 12 or as high as 18 years of age. The definition of sexual activity may range from genital intercourse to various forms of consensual and non-consensual sexual contact.[3]

Prevalence

Sexual abuse of children and adolescents tends to be under-reported. Reasons for this include the limitations mentioned previously as well as reluctance, embarrassment, and shame on the part of the victim. Frequently the perpetrator of the abuse is a family member or someone known and trusted by the family. Fear of reprisal, of disruption of the family, of being blamed, or of not being believed are instrumental in keeping the violation secret. Despite these difficulties researchers are compiling statistics that convey the seriousness of this issue.

A survey of 930 San Franciscan women found that 28% of the women had experienced sexual abuse before the age of 14. Of those women who had been abused, 28% had been victimized by a relative. The rate of abuse increased to 38% when Russell included all abuse before age 17.[4] Finkelhor's 1979 study of 796 college students found that 19% of the females and nine percent of the males had experienced sexual abuse as children.[5] Other studies uncovered sexual abuse rates of 12% for females and 3% for males,[6] 15% females and 6% males,[7] and 10% overall incest rate.[8] Despite the variation in the rates of prevalence reported by various studies, it becomes clear that sexual abuse is occurring to significant numbers of children.

Even using a conservative estimate of prevalence, the number of children presumed to be affected by sexual abuse is shocking. The number of children in the United States is estimated at 60 million, using a sexual abuse prevalence estimate of 10% for females and two percent for males, approximately 7 million of these children will experience sexual abuse before the age of 18.[9] Official reports of sexual abuse incidence provide a more conservative estimate of the number of children who are victims of substantiated reports of sexual abuse each year. The American Humane Association estimated that 71,961 new cases of sexual abuse were reported to state reporting agencies in 1983.[10]

Age of Onset

The greatest risk for sexual abuse appears to be during the pre-adolescent years. The mean age of onset for females is 10 and for males is 11 years of age.[11] However, younger children may not have the cognitive or language skills necessary to report abuse. Finkelhor suggests that age of reporting abuse may be confounded with age of onset of abuse. In a 1988 study, Finkelhor found a relationship between younger age and more severe symptoms in a sample of day-care abuse victims.[12] The Tufts study of 1984 concluded that sexual abuse during the latency period (ages 4 to 11) resulted in the most severe consequences to the victim.[13] Thus, most sexual abuse begins before the victim reaches puberty and this pre-pubescent abuse appears to carry the most severe consequences for the victim.

Gender

The statistics regarding the incidence of sexual abuse by the gender of the victim is showing a decided shift. Earlier statistics indicated the problem to be overwhelmingly female (97%). Recent studies indicate that while females are by far the most frequent victims of sexual abuse (80%), the reported rate of male abuse has increased to 20%.[14] The reasons for the increased rate of reported male sexual abuse may due to greater awareness of the problem within the helping professions. Males may be more reluctant to admit being victims of sexual abuse because of the fear and shame caused by the cultural stigma of homosexuality. Although females are the most frequent victims of sexual abuse, studies suggest that males develop more severe symptoms in response to the abuse.[15]

Perpetrator

Overwhelmingly, the major perpetrators of sexual abuse are male (over 90% of known abusers).[16] In official reports and clinical samples the abuse usually is by a family member or someone known and trusted by the child. A study of 156 victims of sexual abuse referred for treatment reported that 40% of the perpetrators were functioning in the role of parent at the time of the abuse, 47% of the perpetrators lived in the same household, and 33% of the abusers were non-family members. Only 3% of the perpetrators were strangers.[17] Research suggests that the victim experiences greater stress when the perpetrator is a family member.[18] In a study of day-care abuse victims, Finkelhor found that the most severe symptoms developed in children who had been abused by a trusted caretaker.[19] This suggests that the sense of betrayal by a trusted care provider or disruption in the family has more influence than fear of strangers on the adjustment of the victim. Finkelhor also found that stress is greater when the perpetrator is male. In addition, the trauma increased with greater age discrepancy between the victim and the perpetrator.[20]

Although not unanimous, a large number of studies have documented the relationship between the severity of abuse, as measured by violence, and the psychological adjustment of the victim. Children who have experienced violent sexual abuse are apt to exhibit the same symptoms of other trauma victims, such as, physical complaints, psychological disturbances, and behavioral disruptions.[21] The use of violence and aggression appears to have more negative consequences for the victim than more consensual forms of sexual abuse.[22]

Frequency

Several studies have examined the relationship of frequency or duration of abuse and the negative after-effects of abuse; the results are contradictory. The Tufts study of 1984 and Finkelhor did not find a relationship between psychological adjustment of the victim and frequency or duration of the experience.[23] Courois (1979) found the least amount of trauma was associated with the longest duration of sexual contact. Russell's study found an negative association between psychological adjustment and duration of abuse. In a study of day-care abuse victims, Finkelhor found a positive relationship between both frequency of abusive behavior and duration of abusive situation with the severity of symptoms developed by the victim. Although contradictions are apparent, a consensus appears to be emerging which associates longer duration with more negative and longer lasting consequences for the victim.[24]

EFFECTS OF SEXUAL ABUSE

Studies documenting the effects of sexual abuse reveal great variation, from no negative effect to psychotic episodes.[25] A great deal of this variation may be explained by sampling differences; samples taken from clinical settings will exhibit the most severe consequences.

Finkelhor described symptoms of sexual abuse in young children.[26] The initial effects that have been widely noted are fear, anxiety, depression, anger, hostility, aggression, and sexually inappropriate behavior, while the long-term effects most frequently reported are self-destructive behavior, anxiety, feelings of isolation and stigma, poor self-esteem, difficulty in trusting others, a tendency toward substance abuse, maladjustment, and psychological problems. Finkelhor identified several factors that contributed to the severity of the observed symptoms. Supportive family response to the discovery was predictive of lower levels of symptom development. The following characteristics were associated with more severe symptoms: younger age of onset, male victim, male perpetrator, use of coercion or threats, penetration, longer duration, and higher frequency of incidents .

Depression is often reported in clinical samples of child abuse victims.[27] This link has been confirmed in nonclinical samples as well.[28] Anxiety,[29] sexual problems,[30] social adjustment, and substance abuse[31] have all been observed in victims of sexual abuse.

Self-Esteem. The impact of sexual abuse on self-esteem has been studied by several researchers. Bagley and Ramsay found that 19% of the child sexual abuse victims in their random sample scored in the "very poor" category on the Coopersmith Self-Esteem Inventory (versus five percent of the control group), and only nine percent of the victims demonstrated "very good" levels of self-esteem (compared to 20% of the controls).[32] Women with low self-esteem were nearly four times as likely to report a history of child sexual abuse as were the other subjects. Eighty-seven percent of a community sample revealed that their sense of self had been moderately to severely affected by the experience of sexual abuse from a family member.[33] However, 60% of incest victims in a clinical sample reported a negative self-image.[34] While the long-term effects of childhood sexual abuse on the self-esteem of the victims as adults has clearly been established, the immediate or short term link between sexual abuse and self-esteem has not been empirically established.[35] Some children who appear resilient to the negative effects of sexual victimization may develop symptoms related to that experience in later life. High incidence of childhood sexual abuse histories have been discovered in several populations of socially deviant individuals, including juvenile delinquents,[36] prostitutes,[37] and sex offenders.[38] Although these statistics cannot be interpreted to mean that sexual abuse causes social deviancy, there does appear to be a strong association between social deviancy and early victimization.

SEXUAL ABUSE OF RUNAWAYS

Compared to the general population, much higher rates of childhood sexual abuse are noted in studies of specific populations including runaways. Silbert and Pines reported that 60% of runaway prostitutes in their study reported sexual abuse at home prior to running away.[39] Running away is recognized as a sequelae to sexual abuse at home.[40] Female runaways are more likely to be running from sexual abuse (73%) than males (38%).[41]

Tragically, runaways also tend to suffer from sexual abuse and exploitation as a result of living on the street. Sexually abused female runaways are more apt to engage in delinquent activities than non-sexually abused female runaways. This suggests that the experience of sexual abuse, rather than the runaway experience, is predictive of deviant female behavior. It also suggests that sexual abuse characterizes the population of delinquent females.[42] Thus for a significant number of adolescents running away is an attempt to escape an abusive home; yet survival on the street may require the young victims to engage in the very activities from which they were running.

NOTES

1. Russell, D. (1984). Sexual exploitation: *Rape, child sexual abuse, and sexual harassment.* Newbury Park, CA: Sage Publications.

2. National Center on Child Abuse and Neglect (NCCAN). (1981). *Study findings: National study of incidence and severity of child abuse and neglect.* Washington, DC: Department of Health, Education, and Welfare.

3. Russell, D. (1984). *Sexual exploitation: Rape, child sexual abuse, and sexual harassment.* Newbury Park, CA: Sage Publications.

4. Russell, D.E. (1986). *The secret trauma: Incest in the lives of girls and women.* New York: Basic Books.

5. Finkelhor, D. (1979). *Sexually victimized children.* New York: The Free Press.

6. Kercher, G., & McShane, M. (1983). *The prevalence of child sexual abuse victimization in an adult sample of Texas residents.* Huntsville, TX: Sam Houston State University.

7. Finkelhor, D. (1986). *A source book on child sexual abuse. Newbury Park,* CA: Sage Publications, Inc.

8. Gordon, L., O'Keefe, P. (1985). The "normality" of incest. In A.W. Burgess (Ed.), *Rape and sexual assault* (pp. 70-82). New York: Garland Publishing.

9. Finkelhor, D. (1986). *A source book on child sexual abuse.* Newbury Park, CA: Sage Publications, Inc.

10. American Association for Protecting Children. (1986). *Highlights of official child neglect and abuse reporting,* 1984. Denver: American Humane Association.

11. Finkelhor, D. (1984). *Child sexual abuse: New theories and research.* New York: Free Press.

12. Finkelhor, D. (1988). *Nursery crimes.* Newbury Park, CA: Sage.

13. Tufts New England Medical Center Study. (1984). Final report to the Department of Juvenile Justice and Delinquency Prevention. (Sexual Abuse Treatment Project at Tufts.) Boston, MA: New England Medical Center.

14. Conte, J.R. (1984). Progress in treating the sexual abuse of children. *Social Work,* 258-263.

15. Finkelhor, D. (1988). *Nursery crimes.* Newbury Park, CA: Sage.

16. Russell, D.E. (1986). *The secret trauma: Incest in the lives of girls and women.* New York: Basic Books.

17. Gomes-Schwartz, B., Horowitz, J.M., & Cardarelli, A.P. (1990). *Child sexual abuse.* Newbury Park, CA: Sage Publications.

18. Russell, D.E. (1984). *Sexual exploitation: Rape. Child sexual abuse and workplace harassment.* Newbury Park, CA: Sage Publications, Inc.

19. Finkelhor, D. (1988). *Nursery crimes.* Newbury Park, CA: Sage.

20. Finkelhor, D. (1979). Sexually victimized children. New York: The Free Press.

21. Hartman, C.R., & Burgess, A.W. (1986). Child sexual abuse: Generic roots of the victim experience. *Journal of Psychotherapy and the Family,* 2(2), 83-92.

22. Finkelhor, D. (1979). *Sexually victimized children.* New York: The Free Press.

23. Finkelhor, D. (1979). *Sexually victimized children.* New York: The Free Press.

24. Gomes-Schwartz, B., Horowitz, J.M., & Cardarelli, A.P. (1990). *Child sexual abuse.* Newbury Park, CA: Sage Publications.

25. Cicchetti, D., & Carlson, V. (1989). *Child maltreatment: Theory and research on the causes and consequences of child abuse and neglect.* Cambridge, MA: Cambridge University Press.

26. Finkelhor, D. (1988). *Nursery crimes*. Newbury Park, CA: Sage.

27. Finkelhor, D. (1986). *A source book on child sexual abuse*. Newbury Park, CA: Sage Publications, Inc.

28. Sedney, M.A., & Brooks, B. (1984). Factors associated with a history of childhood sexual experience in a nonclinical female population. *Journal of American Academy of Child Psychiatry*, 23, 215-218.

29. Briere, J. (1984). *The effects of childhood sexual abuse on later psychological functioning: Defining a "post-sexual-abuse syndrome."* Paper presented at the third national Conference on Sexual Victimization of Children, Washington, DC.

30. Meiselman, K. (1979). *Incest: A psychiatric study of causes and effects with treatment recommendations*. San Francisco: Jossey-Bass.

31. Peters, S.D. (1984). *The relationship between childhood sexual victimization and adult depression among Afro-American and White women*. Unpublished doctoral dissertation, University of California, Los Angeles.

32. Bagley, C., & Ramsay, R. (1985). *Disrupted childhood and vulnerability to sexual assault: Long-term sequels with implications for counseling*. Paper presented at the Conference on Counselling the Sexual Abuse Survivor, Winnipeg.

33. Courois, C. (1979). The incest experience and its aftermath. *Victimology: An International Journal*, 4, 337-347.

34. Herman, J.A. (1981). *Father-daughter incest*. Cambridge, MA: Harvard University Press.

35. Finkelhor, D. (1986). *A source book on child sexual abuse*. Newbury Park, CA: Sage Publications, Inc.

36. Reich, J.W., & Gutierre, S.E. (1979). Escape/aggression incidence in sexually abused juvenile delinquents. *Criminal Justice and Behavior*, 6, 239-243.

37. Silbert, M.H., & Pines, A.M. (1981). Sexual child abuse as an antecedent to prostitution. *Child Abuse and Neglect*, 5, 407-411.

38. Groth, A.N. (1978). Patterns of sexual assault against children and adolescents. In A.W. Burgess, A.N. Groth, L.L. Homstrom, & S.M. Sgroi (Eds.), *Sexual assault of children and adolescents*. Lexington, MA: Lexington Books.

39. Silbert, M.H., & Pines, A.M. (1981). Sexual child abuse as an antecedent to prostitution. *Child Abuse and Neglect*, 5, 407-411.

40. Summit, R. (1983). The child abuse accommodation syndrome. *Child Abuse and Neglect: The International Journal*, 7(2), 177-193.

41. Janus, M.D., McCormack, A., Burgess, A.W., & Hartman, C. (1987). *Adolescent runaways: Causes and consequences.* Lexington, MA: Lexington Books.

42. McCormack, A., Janus, M.D., & Burgess, A.W. (1986). Runaway youths and sexual victimization: Gender differences in an adolescent runaway population. *Child Abuse and Neglect*, 10, 387-395.

IV
Runaway Study: Methods and Procedures

This chapter describes the sample and procedures used in this research. The study was conducted at a shelter in Toronto, Canada, in 1987. The participants in the study were runaways who sought shelter at Convent House in the summer of 1987. The purpose of the study was to reliably record the incidence and nature of physical and sexual abuse among adolescent runaways. In 1990, an additional sample of adolescents at a small urban high school in Connecticut was administered the Rosenberg Self-Esteem Inventory.

METHODOLOGY

Procedure

Runaways seeking services at a Canadian shelter for homeless and runaway adolescents were asked by staff members if they would be willing to be interviewed concerning their experiences prior to running away, reasons for running away, and experiences after running away from home. The youths were informed that the interview would be conducted by persons not employed by the shelter, their responses would be confidential, the information would not be shared with shelter staff, and they could withdraw from the interview at any time. For those who agreed to participate, an appointment was scheduled for the next day, the purpose of the research was re-explained, and a consent form was signed.

Three non-staff interviewers were trained to administer the Archambault and Janus Interview Schedule which was specially designed for this study.[1] The semi-structured interview took approximately one and one-half hours to conduct. A total of 195 interviews were completed between June and August of 1987.

Additionally, self-esteem data were collected from high school students to serve as a comparison for the data from the runaways. The high school student data were collected in 1990 at a small urban school (n = 153) and at a rural high school (n = 20) in the northeastern United States. After describing the purpose of the study, classroom teachers asked students to volunteer to anonymously complete the questionnaire. The teachers told the students that they did not have to participate and that they were not to identify themselves on the questionnaire.

Instrumentation

Rosenberg Self-Esteem Inventory. The Rosenberg Self-Esteem Inventory (RSE) is a 10-item scale developed by Morris Rosenberg to measure global self-acceptance.[2] This scale was developed for use with high school students. The scale has a four-point response format ranging from "Strongly Disagree" to "Strongly Agree." Scores are derived from a hierarchical combination of responses that are consistent with self-acceptance. A low score of one indicates the lowest level of self-acceptance, while a high score of six indicates the highest level of self-acceptance.

Validity of the Rosenberg Self-Esteem Inventory was documented by Byrne and Shavelson. They presented evidence of convergent and discriminant validities in a multitrait-multimethod matrix by demonstrating that RSE correlates more highly with other measures of self-esteem than with other unrelated measures.[3] Construct validity evidence may be inferred from the range of theoretically predicted associations that have been demonstrated: depressive affect, anxiety, psychosomatic symptoms, interpersonal insecurity, leadership, and parental disinterest. Reported internal consistency reliabilities range from .77 to .87.[4] Test-retest reliability have been estimated at .85.[5] The internal consistency reliability of RSE for the high school sample in this study was .84 and for the runaways it was .85. Thus, the RSE demonstrates satisfactory internal consistency for both the runaways and the high school students in this study.

Archambault-Janus Interview Schedule. The Archambault-Janus Interview Schedule (AJIS) is a specially designed 90-minute, semi-structured interview schedule which provides information on the characteristics of runaways, the reasons they ran away, the nature and type of physical abuse they experienced both in the home prior to running away and on the street after running away, and the nature and type of sexual abuse they experienced. The AJIS is arranged so that demographic data are gathered first, followed by the more sensitive physical and sexual abuse information, and then the less sensitive self-esteem data. The definition of physical abuse used by Straus and Gelles[6] is adapted for use in this study. Figure 2 presents the behavioral experiences and definitions of abuse used in this study and their relationship to the Straus and Gelles definitions. The youths were interviewed about the occurrence of any of the behavioral experiences, age at first occurrence, age at last occurrence, frequency, and perpetrator of each of these behaviors, first while at home and then while on the street. Each youth's responses were then scaled on the level of physical abuse ranging from No Violence to Very Severe Violence (see Figure 2).

The part of the interview that addresses sexual abuse follows the physical abuse section. Information was gathered about how the runaways first learned about sex and their first sexual experience. The adolescents were asked if they had ever had sex with a relative and, if so, who it was. Questions were asked about: sex with an authority figure, unwanted sexual experiences, violent sexual experiences, rape, pornography, prostitution, and hustling. The AJIS does not consistently ask about age of onset, frequency, severity, and perpetrator for the sexual experiences. Therefore, there are missing data in these variables and the estimates may not be as stable as in the physical abuse section where questions about age of onset, frequency, severity, and perpetrator of abuse are asked consistently.

Two trained scorers assessed the interviews and rated the two responses about first sexual experiences. The scorers achieved 100% agreement on the presence of abuse rating. Abuse was defined by the presence of the criteria listed in the sexual abuse section. Three additional scorers, experienced in either psychometrics or child abuse, were trained to code the interview. The scorers were trained and supervised until an minimum inter-rater reliability of .85 was achieved. Retraining was implemented for scorers if inter-rater reliabilities dropped below .85. Overall inter-rater reliability was .91.

Sample

The runaway sample consisted of 195 homeless runaway youths between the ages of 16 and 20 (mdn = 18), who received services at Covenant House, Toronto, in the summer of 1987.

Figure 2
Comparison of Abuse Definitions

Behaviors	Welsh	Straus
A. Minor Violence Acts (M)		
1. Threw something	M	M
2. Pushed		M
3. Grabbed/shoved	M	M
4. Slapped or spanked		M
5. Denied food/clothes/ school/medical	M	
6. Pulled muscle from fight	M	
7. Tried to hit with object	M	S
B. Severe Violence Acts* (S)		
8. Repeatedly slapped	S	
9. Hit with object that left: Mark/bruise/welt/cut	S	S
10. Tied up/rope burns	S	
11. Injured or had difficulty walking/sitting	S	
12. Threatened with gun/weapon	S	S
C. Very Severe Violence Acts* (VS)		
13. Kicked/bit/hit with fist	VS	VS
14. Beat up/punched	VS	VS
15. Used gun or weapon	VS	VS
16. Head banged	VS	
17. Choked		VS
18. Burned/scalded	VS	VS
19. Held under water	VS	
20. Injured-Hospital	VS	
D. Violence Indices		
Overall Violence (1 - 20)		
Severe Violence* (8 - 12)		
Very Severe Violence* (13 - 20)		

* Defined as abuse.

Table 2 provides a breakdown of the age at the time of the interview for males (mdn = 18) and females (mdn = 17) separately. The females who were interviewed for this study were approximately a year younger than the males in this study. Females comprised 39.5% (n = 77) of the sample, while males comprised 60.5% (n = 118) of the sample. This figure is consistent with gender representation in other studies of runaways.[7]

Table 2
Age of Runaways at Time of Interview

Age	Total		Male		Female	
	n	%	n	%	n	%
16	32	16.4	11	9.3	21	27.3
17	44	22.6	23	19.5	21	27.3
18	51	26.2	34	28.8	17	22.0
19	33	16.9	28	23.7	5	6.5
20	35	17.9	22	18.6	13	16.9
Total	195		118		77	

Ethnic characteristics of the sample are presented in Table 3. Analyses by ethnic groups were not appropriate because of the low number of minority runaways, as well as the fact that this is a sample of Canadian runaways whose ethnic population patterns are different from those in the United States. Other studies also have found a high proportion of white runaway youths.[8] Many studies of runaways find their subjects at agencies such as Covenant House. No studies have investigated whether there is a lower incidence of running away among minority youth or if minority runaways are less apt to contact agencies. However, it is interesting to note that the percent of female minority runaways is double that of male minority runaways.

Table 4 shows that 77% of the sample left home for the first time after the age of 14. An interesting pattern emerges when examining age of first running away for males and females separately. A full third of the females left home for the first time before the age of 14, while less than a fifth of the males left home that young. Of those reporting first runaway episode after the age of 14, only 34% were

Table 3
Ethnicity of Runaway Adolescents

Race	Total n	%	Male n	%	Female n	%
White	161	82.6	103	87.3	58	75.3
Black	20	9.7	5	4.2	15	19.5
Hispanic	6	3.1	3	2.5	3	3.9
Asian	1	0.5	1	0.8	0	0.0
Other	7	4.0	6	5.1	1	1.3
All Minorities	34	17.4	15	12.7	19	24.7
Total	195		118		77	

Table 4
Age First Left Home

Ages	Total Sample Total n	%	Male n	%	Female n	%	Percentage In Age Group % Male	Female
6 - 10	10	5.1	5	4.2	5	6.5	50.0	50.0
11 - 13	35	17.9	14	11.9	21	27.3	40.0	60.0
14 +	150	76.9	99	83.9	51	66.2	66.0	34.0

female Thus, in this sample, females had a pronounced tendency to run away at a younger age than males.

Running away was a multiple occurrence for nearly three-quarters of the sample (See Table 5). The tendency toward multiple occurrences of running away is greater for females (82%) than for males (66%). However, some of the adolescents reported having run away from different homes. One runaway indicated that she had run away four times; she left her father's house once, a cousin's house once, and had "lived off and on the street". A male, who reported running away once, indicated that when he was 5 or 6 years old he had run away from three foster homes trying to return to a previous foster home, but he did not count that as running away. Another runaway who reported running away one time described her runaway experiences, "The Children's Aid Society removed me (from home) after the police took me home. I have run away from different group homes, foster homes about 75 times." Therefore, the number of times the adolescents report running away may be an underestimate of the actual disruption in their lives. Although not consistent, the runaways seem to describe running away as leaving the home of a relative, but not describing leaving a placement as running away.

Actual amount of time living on the streets was not available in this data set, but time exposed to street life was calculated by subtracting age of first running away from age at the time of the interview. The majority of these youths had been in and out of their homes since they first ran away, as evidenced by the multiple occurrences of running away. This measure of amount of time exposed to street life is a measure of the time in turmoil, alternating between home and street life. The median time since first running away was three years for both males and females.

Table 5
Frequency of Running Away

Number of Times	Total		Male		Female	
	n	%	n	%	n	%
Isolated Occurrence	52	26.6	39	33.0	13	17.0
2 - 10 Times	120	61.5	67	56.7	53	68.0
11+ Times	23	11.8	12	10.2	11	14.0

Table 6 presents information about the high school sample. The sample consisted of 173 high school students from either a small American urban school (n = 153) or an American rural school (n = 20). Information was not gathered from the high school sample concerning abuse or runaway history. These students ranged from 14 to 19 years old. The high school sample comprised 50% of youths 16 or younger, while the runaway sample comprised only 16% of youths 16 or younger. Thus, the high school sample represents a younger group of American adolescents, while the runaway sample represents an older Canadian group of adolescents.

Table 6
High School Students

Age	Total n	%	Male n	%	Female n	%
14	9	5.2	6	7.2	3	3.4
15	30	17.3	14	16.9	16	18.0
16	48	27.7	19	22.9	29	32.6
17	59	34.1	28	33.7	30	33.7
18	25	14.5	15	18.1	10	11.2
19	2	1.2	1	1.2	1	1.1
Total	173		83		89	

Note. Missing data result in discrepancies in totals.

VARIABLES IN THE STUDY

This section describes the operational definition of each of the variables. Some variables are composites, or combinations, of single variables or items.

Self-Esteem

Self-esteem is defined as a sense of self-acceptance. Self-esteem scores are the sum of the responses to the 10 items on the RSE. Responses have been recoded, when necessary, so that a high score on the RSE indicates high self-esteem. The latent variable of self-esteem is indicated by the 10 responses to the RSE. In the runaway sample, self-esteem data were gathered during an interview. Whereas, in the high school sample, self-esteem data were reported on a paper and pencil inventory. While these differences in data collection methods and sample characteristics are a concern, the additional comparison between these groups of adolescents is informative.

Physical Abuse

Physical Abuse at Home. Physical abuse at home is the self-report of violent experiences that occurred while living at home. The runaways' responses to specific behaviors (see Figure 2) were gathered after the following statement was read: "One of the reasons some kids leave home is that they are physically abused. I'm going to read you a list of the things we mean by physical abuse. Have any of these things ever happened to you at home?" The latent variable Physical Abuse at Home was estimated using the indices described in Figure 2.

Age of Onset of Abuse. The runaways were asked the age that each experience first occurred. The age of onset is the minimum age of any type of reported abusive behaviors. Age of onset was divided into early childhood (1 to 6 years), childhood (7 to 11 years), early adolescence (12 to 15 years), or adolescence (16 to 20 years).

Child Abuse. Child abuse is defined as abusive behavior towards children younger than 12 years of age.

Adolescent Abuse. Adolescent abuse is defined as abusive behavior towards children between 12 and 20 years old.

Frequency. Each youth was asked the number of times the behavior occurred. Frequency, in this study, is defined across abusive incidents rather than within incidents. Since several types of violent behaviors typically occurred in a single incident, it was determined that the maximum of any single abusive behavior would provide a conservative estimate of the frequency of physical abuse. Frequency of physical abuse was collapsed in four categories: Isolated or Rare (1 to 2 times), Infrequent (3 to 10 times), Frequent (11 to 99 times), and Very Frequent (100 or more times).

Severity. Severity of abuse is determined by the specific type of abuse reported (See Figure 2).

Very Severe Violence. Very severe violence is defined as one or more of the following: being kicked, being punched, having head banged on the floor or wall, being injured to require hospital visit, being assaulted with a weapon, being intentionally burned, or being held under water.

Severe Violence. Severe violence is defined as one or more of the following: being injured in a way that resulted in difficulty walking or sitting, being repeatedly slapped, being hit with an object that left a mark, bruise, cut, or welt, being tied up, being threatened with a gun or weapon, or being given rope burns.

Minor Violence. Minor violence is defined as one or more of the following: having an object thrown at you, being grabbed and thrown around, being denied food, clothes, or access to school or medical attention; or being in a fight that resulted in a pulled muscle. In this study, minor violence is not defined as abuse.

The categories of physical abuse are exclusive, that is, a person who suffered severe violence and very severe violence will be included in only the very severe violence category. The category will represent the most severe type of abuse experienced.

Relationship of Perpetrator. The runaways were asked to identify who did this to them for each specific type of violence reported. The perpetrator in this study is the person who was cited the most frequently; thus it is a measure of the primary perpetrator of abuse. Closeness of relationship is coded as caretaker (mother, father, stepmother, stepfather, and grandparent) and other (sibling, stepsibling, cousin, aunt, uncle, mother's friend, father's friend, and other).

Physical Abuse on the Street. Physical abuse on the street is the self-report of violent experiences that occurred while living on the streets after leaving home. Each runaway's responses to 20 specific behaviors (See Figure 2) were gathered after the following statement was read: "Some kids who run away from home are physically abused while they are on the streets (running away). I'd like to read the list of things we mean by physical abuse and have you tell me whether any of these things happened to you while you were running away (on the streets)." The latent variable *Physical Abuse on the Street* was estimated by four indicators of physical abuse on the street. The definitions of age of onset of abuse, frequency of abuse, severity of abuse, and relationship of primary caretaker are the same as for physical abuse at home.

Sexual Abuse

Sexual abuse is defined by the presence of one of the following criteria:[9]

1. report of the presence of force, threat, or coercion;
2. age discrepancy (five years for subjects younger than 14, 10 years for subjects 14 or older);
3. age inappropriateness of experience (cunnilingus, anilingus, intercourse, and sodomy before the age of 14); or
4. presence of illegal activity, such as prostitution or pornography.

Runaways were asked to tell about seven specific potentially abusive experiences. They were asked about having:

1. their first sexual experience;
2. sex with someone much older than themselves;
3. sex with a relative (siblings, stepsiblings, and cousins were omitted from the definition due to difficulty in determining the presence of abuse);
4. unwanted sexual advances by someone with authority over them;
5. sex with someone they didn't want to have sex with;
6. sex where there was violence or the threat of violence, or where they were afraid of being sexually assaulted;
7. been raped; or
8. been involved with hustling or prostitution.

Therefore, there are eight possible abusive sexual experiences in this study.

Severity of Sexual Experience. Severity of the experience was defined by Russell's three categories of severity of abuse.[10]

1. Russell 1 (Least Severe-Body Violation) is defined as completed or attempted acts of intentional touching of buttocks, thigh, leg, or other body part, clothed breasts or genitals, or kissing; forced or unforced.
2. Russell 2 (Severe-Genital Violation) is defined as completed or attempted genital fondling, simulated intercourse, or digital penetration; both forced and unforced.
3. Russell 3 (Most Severe-Penetration) is defined as completed or attempted vaginal, oral, or anal intercourse, cunnilingus, or anilingus; forced or unforced.

Age of Onset. Age of onset is the self-reported age of first occurrence of any of the behaviors that are defined as abusive or violent. Severity at first occurrence is not a factor when estimating age of onset. Age of onset was divided into early childhood (1 to 6 years), childhood (7 to 11 years), early adolescence (12 to 15 years), or adolescence (16 to 20 years).

Frequency. Frequency is the self-reported number of times that the experience occurred. Frequency of sexual abuse was collapsed in four categories: Isolated or Rare (1 to 2 times), Infrequent (3 to 9 times), Frequent (10 to 49 times), and Very Frequent (50 or more times). Frequency is not summative across all abusive situations, rather it is the number of occurrences of the most frequently occurring type of abuse.

Relationship of Perpetrator. The perpetrator is determined by the runaway's response to the question, "Who did this to you?" The perpetrator in this study is the person who was cited the most frequently; thus it is a measure of the primary perpetrator of abuse. Closeness of relationship is coded as caretaker (mother, father, stepmother, stepfather, and grandparent) and other (aunt, uncle, mother's friend, father's friend, and other). Definitional difficulties in categorization of behaviors as abusive related to brother, sister, stepbrother, stepsister, and cousin resulted in the elimination of these relatives from the analysis. Thus, the estimation of sexual abuse is conservative and may be an underestimate of actual sexual abuse.

DATA ANALYSES

This section is designed to provide an overview of the statistical procedures that were employed to analyze the data and address the research questions.

Data Screening

The data were screened for out-of-range responses and outliers, and were analyzed for skewness/normality, linearity, and homogeneity of variance. Out-of-range responses were identified through frequency tables. Univariate outliers were identified through scattergrams and z-scores ($z > 3$). Mahalanabois distances and residuals were examined for multivariate outliers. Normality and skewness were analyzed using frequency distributions and the skewness statistic. Linearity of the data was tested through SPSSX Means procedure. Homogeneity of variance was tested with the Bartlett-Box test.

Missing Data. Cases which reported the occurrence of a type of abuse (physical abuse at home, physical abuse on the street, or sexual abuse), but did not provide information about the nature of the abuse (age of onset, frequency, severity or relationship of perpetrator) were coded as missing. Missing and non-missing cases were analyzed for differences on the Rosenberg Self-Esteem Inventory (RSE). The t-tests between missing and non-missing cases with respect to RSE revealed no significant differences. This provided evidence that there was no relationship between non-response to these variables and self-esteem. This suggested that the reasons the runaways did not respond to the questions were unrelated to their self-esteem. However, the variable "relationship of perpetrator" presented several problems. The fact that only 16 of the 195 runaways chose to identify the perpetrator of sexual abuse and the lack of variance in the perpetrators of physical abuse at home (96% caretaker) and on the street (94% other) led the researcher to eliminate relationship of perpetrator from further analyses in this study. Responses from the runaways who volunteered to be interviewed but did not respond to the RSE were analyzed for differences in type and characteristics of abuse. Results of the frequency distributions revealed that while responses from these cases often were missing on several variables, they demonstrated similarity on the reported variables. Thus, elimination of these cases from the final analysis should not bias the results.

Distributions. Two variables (frequency of street abuse and frequency of sexual abuse) were significantly positively skewed. This indicated that more cases than expected were found in the lower part of the distribution. Recommended transformations were performed to evaluate whether the transformed variables improved the prediction.[11] Since none of these transformations resulted in improved explanation of RSE (using multiple regression), the original untransformed variables were used in the analyses.

Outliers. Standard scores were analyzed to determine univariate outliers ($z > 3$). Eleven univariate outliers were identified; these cases were dropped from the study because of extreme scores on variables, such as age or self-esteem. Mahalanabois distances were evaluated to detect multivariate outliers. Two cases were identified as multivariate outliers and dropped from the analysis. This resulted in a final sample of 176 runaways, 107 males and 69 females.

Linearity. SPSSX procedure Means was used to evaluate the data for a linear relationship with RSE. This procedure provided a significance test for the nonlinear component of the analysis. No significant nonlinearity was found.

Descriptive Statistics

Frequency analyses were run to obtain means and standard deviations of the four indicators (age of onset, frequency, severity, and closeness of relationship of perpetrator) of the three latent abuse variables (physical abuse at home, physical abuse on the street and sexual abuse) and of total self-esteem score. Frequencies were produced for the total sample and separately for males and females.

Correlations were computed between total score on RSE and the four indicators (age of onset, frequency, severity, and closeness of relationship of perpetrator) of the three latent abuse variables (physical abuse at home, physical abuse on the street, and sexual abuse). Descriptive statistics were used to determine the nature and characteristics of physical and sexual abuse experienced by adolescent runaways.

Inferential Statistics

Analysis of variance. Analysis of variance was used to:
1. compare high school students' and runaways' responses to the Rosenberg Self-Esteem Inventory to determine if, as a group, runaways differ from high school students with respect to level of self-esteem;
2. examine differences in self-esteem among runaways who experienced different types of abuse (physical, sexual, both physical and sexual, and none);
3. investigate the relationship between frequency of abuse and self-esteem in both male and female runaways.

Structural Equation Modeling

Structural equation modeling (SEM) involves specification of a theoretical measurement and structural model, estimation and testing the model, and modification or respecification of the model.[12] Model specification is based on theory, thus model testing is confirmatory. Model respecification and modification are based on a combination of theory and data analysis; thus model respecification is exploratory. Figure 3 represents the theoretical model; latent variables are represented by circles. Indicators of the latent variables are denoted X1

Figure 3
Theoretical Model of Relationships Among Physical Abuse, Sexual Abuse, and Self-Esteem

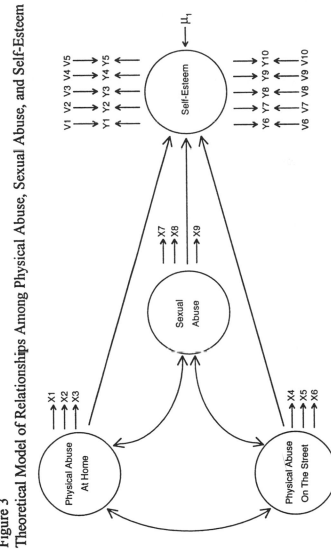

Note. X1, X4, and X7 = Age of Onset; X2, X5, and X8 = Frequency; X3, X6, and X9 = Severity. Y1 to Y10 = Items on Rosenberg Self-esteem Inventory. V1 to V10 = Measurement error. μ₁ = Disturbance.

to X9. The direction of the relationships among the variables are denoted by one-headed arrows. Arrows point from hypothesized independent variables (exogenous) to hypothesized dependent variables (endogenous). In this study, physical abuse at home, physical abuse on the street, and sexual abuse are exogenous latent variables, while self-esteem is the endogenous latent variable. Curved arrows indicate hypothesized correlation among exogenous variables, but the direction of the relationships are not indicated. The part of the endogenous variable that is not explained by the variables in the model are called the disturbance (error).

Each latent variable is presumed to be an underlying cause of a set of measured or observed variables. An arrow pointing from a latent variable to a measured variable (X) indicates an assumption that individuals' positions on the latent variable are indicated by their responses to the measured variables. In this study each exogenous variable is measured or indicated by recollections of four specific characteristics of the abuse: age of onset, severity, frequency, and closeness of the relationship of by an arrow leading from the error term to the indicator.

Structural equation modeling was used to determine:

1. how much of the runaways' self-esteem could be explained by their experiences of physical and sexual abuse, and
2. whether the pattern of interrelations is the same for males and females.

This chapter described the methods and procedures used to conduct this study. The research design, definition of variables, and research questions are explained. The sampling procedures, data collection methods, and sample of subjects was presented. The instruments and their psychometric properties were discussed. The chapter concluded with a description of the analyses used to answer the research questions.

NOTES

1. Archambault, F.X., & Janus, M.D. (1987). *Physical and sexual abuse: A runaway interview schedule.* Unpublished manuscript, University of Connecticut, Bureau of Educational Research, Storrs.

2. Rosenberg, M. (1965). Society and adolescent self-image. Princeton, NJ: Princeton University Press.

3. Byrne, B.M., & Shavelson, R.J. (1986). On the structure of adolescent self-concept. Journal of Educational Psychology, 78, 474-481.

4. Wylie, R.C. (1989). Measures of self-concept. Lincoln: University of Nebraska Press.

5. Sibler, E., & Tippett, J.S. (1965). Self-esteem: Clinical assessment and measurement validation. Psychological Reports, 16, 1017-1071.

6. Straus, M., & Gelles, R. (1989). Physical violence in American families. New Brunswick, NJ: Transaction Publishers.

7. McCormack, A., Janus, M.D., & Burgess, A.W. (1986). Runaway youths and sexual victimization: Gender differences in an adolescent runaway population. Child Abuse and Neglect, 10, 387-395.

8. Farber, E., Kinast, C., McCoard, W., & Falkner, D. (1984). Violence in families of adolescent runaways. Child Abuse and Neglect, 8(3), 295-299.

9. Janus, M., Archambault, F.X., & Welsh, L.A. (1988). Physical and sexual abuse in runaway homeless youth. Paper presented at the 96th annual meeting of the American Psychological Association, Atlanta, GA.

10. Russell, D.E. (1984). Sexual exploitation: Rape. Child sexual abuse and workplace harassment. Newbury Park, CA: Sage Publications, Inc.

11. Tabachnick, B.G., & Fidell, L.S. (1989). *Using multivariate statistics*. New York: Harper Collins.

12. Joreskog, K., & Sorbom, D. (1986). LISREL: Analysis of linear structural relationships by the method of maximum likelihood. Morresville, IN: Scientific Software.

V
Running Away and Physical Abuse

This chapter describes the runaways, their reasons for running away, and the physical abuse they experienced both at home and on the street.

RUNNING AWAY

At the beginning of the interview the runaways were asked to talk about their reasons for running away and to describe their experiences while running away. Thirty-nine percent of the runaways indicated that when they first ran away their mothers and fathers were married. However, only 29% of the adolescents were living with both their parents.

Reasons for Leaving Home for the First Time

The runaways were asked about the reasons for leaving home the first time and the last time they left. The interviewer said, "We think there are some reasons why kids run away from home. I want you to think back and tell me whether these were important reasons for you leaving home the first (or last) time. Table 7 displays the reasons the runaways indicated were important in their decision to leave home the first time. The reasons considered important by the highest percentage of runaways were not getting along with the male (57%) or female (57%) in the home or feeling unloved (56%). The next most important reasons cited were being physically abused (40%) and being thrown out (38%) of the house. Physical abuse was cited by significantly more ($\chi 2 = 5.18$) females (49%) than males (33%), as well as sexual abuse ($\chi 2 = 16.72$), and conflict with the female adult ($\chi 2 = 6.72$).

One female reported running away at age 16 because "I felt left out and unattached. Dad never gave me credit; he put me down."

Another runaway reported, "My Mom was totally unreasonable. She wouldn't even listen to my side of the story." Another runaway told the interviewer that her parents had separated and her mother had moved in with a boyfriend. She felt that they didn't care about her and that the boyfriend was more important to her mother. When her mother and boyfriend moved to the country she wanted to stay in the city and go to school.

A female, who indicated that sexual abuse was an important reason for leaving said, "my mother married my Uncle; I used to think he was my father. I left when he started making passes at me." Another female who reported sexual abuse as a reason for leaving said, "I left because my parents trusted their friend and didn't believe me when I told them he had raped me."

Table 7

Reasons for Leaving Home the First Time

| Reasons | Percent Endorsing Reason[a] | | |
	Males (n = 118)	Females (n = 77)	Total (n = 195)
Physical Abuse*	33	49	40
Sexual Abuse **	4	24	12
Thrown Out	38	37	38
Excessive Drinking (male adult)[b]	26	23	25
Excessive Drinking (female adult)[b]	11	18	14
Drug Use (male adult)	5	12	8
Drug Use (female adult)	5	13	8
Conflict (male adult)	55	61	57
Conflict (female adult)	50	69	57
Feeling Unloved	53	62	56

a. Percent of respondents citing reasons rounded to the nearest whole percent.

b. Adult males include father, stepfather, or mother's friend; female adults include mother, stepmother, or father's friend.

* Indicates significant differences between males and females at .05 level.

** Indicates significant differences at .01 level.

Table 8
Reasons for Leaving Home First and Last Times Combined

Reasons	Percent Endorsing Reason[a]	
	Either Time	Both Times
Physical Abuse	50	26
Sexual Abuse	15	7
Thrown Out	60	32
Excessive Drinking (male adult)[b]	30	12
Excessive Drinking (female adult)[b]	19	10
Drug Use (male adult)	10	6
Drug Use (female adult)	13	8
Conflict (male adult)	69	46
Conflict (female adult)	68	47
Feeling Unloved	60	43

a. Percentage rounded to nearest whole percent.
b. Adult males include father, stepfather, or mother's friend; female adults include mother, stepmother, or father's friend.

The adolescents were asked for the important reasons for leaving home the last time. The first column of Table 8 displays the percentage of runaways who indicated the reasons either the first or last time. The second column indicates the percentage of adolescents who cited the same reason both the first and last time they left home. Fifty percent or more of the runaways cited physical abuse, conflict with male or female adult, getting thrown out, and feeling unloved as important reasons for leaving home either the first or last times they left home. While conflict with male and female adults and feeling unloved were the most likely to be cited as reasons for leaving home both times.

Runaways not citing physical abuse (or other reasons) for running away, may still have experienced physical abuse at home. For example, one runaway, who did not indicate that physical abuse was a reason for running away, later reported (a) being punched with a fist (once), (b) being kicked (3 times), (c) being repeatedly slapped (20 or more times), (d) being hit so hard it left bruises, cuts or welts and made walking difficult (20) or more times, (e) being denied food (50 or more times), and (f) being denied medical attention when he had a hernia at age 6. He reported difficulty in getting along with male and female caretakers, feeling unloved, and being thrown out of the house as important reasons for leaving home. Therefore, caution must be exercised when interpreting the reasons for leaving home. Adolescents may have had very negative experiences that they do not cite as reasons for running away.

Fourteen females (18%) and four males (3%) reported that both physical and sexual abuse were important reasons for running away. Thus, early in the interview, 9% of the sample indicated that they had left home because they were victims of both physical and sexual abuse. Later, the runaways are asked about specific behaviors that are considered abusive.

Runaways who reported being thrown out of the house were asked to explain why they were thrown out. One runaway reported, "I didn't see things the way my mother did. I lived in Jamaica with my grandmother until three years ago when I came to live here. I was really different from who she (her mother) wanted me to be." Another adolescent reported, "I wasn't getting along with my mother. We couldn't communicate and my mother was always hitting me. We had a fight, as always, and I was thrown out." Another runaway indicated she was thrown out because she did not go to school. A male said, "I don't really understand. My parents were tired of all the kids, but I was the oldest. I was 16 and could be kicked out, the others were still too young." A 16 year old female explains that she was kicked out because she spent the money her parents gave her for an abortion and lied about it.

Some of the runaways talked about returning home. One female, who was having trouble dealing with her parents' separation, her mother's affair, and her mother's boyfriend, said she would like to go home because of money and missing her Mom. She would like to be in a family again, but not under the present conditions. A male said he would like to go back, but it would just be the same. They would still disregard his feelings and opinions. They would say he was just a kid. "My parents appear to care, but they don't really. All of the kids (2 younger brothers and 2 younger sisters) feel unloved. My parents say I'm the one, I don't feel the love that they give, but none of the kids feel loved." A female was planning on returning home after she had an abortion because her cat just had kittens and she wanted to see them.

One young woman, who was removed from her home because her father was sexually abusing her, said she could never go home because her father would probably kill her for telling. Another runaway was afraid to go home because she had hit her mother during the last fight. "I'm not a violent person, I don't know what went on there. I'm afraid if I go home I'll do it again, we fight all the time." Another runaway reported that both her parents beat her. "My mother says she'll beat me before my father does so that it won't be so bad."

PHYSICAL ABUSE

Each youth was interviewed about the types and amount of physical violence they had experienced before leaving home and while living on the streets. The interviewer said, "One of the reasons some kids leave home is that they are physically abused. I'm going to read you a list of the things we mean by physical abuse. Have any of these things ever happened to you?" After the list was completed the interviewer said, "Some kids who run away from home are also physically abused while they are running away (on the street). I'd like you to read again the list of things we mean by physical abuse and tell me whether any of these things happened to you while you were running away (on the street).

Table 9 displays the rate of overall occurrence of abuse among the runaway sample. The adolescents who reported Severe or Very severe acts of violence are defined as "abused" in this study. The highest incidence of abuse occurred for physical abuse at home (81%). Females had a somewhat higher rate of physical abuse at home (83%), although males, by no means, were immune (791%). Physical abuse on the street, contrary to popular belief, was less likely (65%) than at home, at least for this sample of runaways. Males (67%) were more likely to be victims of street violence than females (61%).

Physical Abuse at Home

Table 10 summarizes the findings of physical violence at home by specific descriptions of behavior. The specific violent behaviors that were most likely for this sample were having something thrown at them (58%), being hit with something that left a mark, bruise or welt (56%), and being beaten up or punched (56%) or being grabbed and thrown around (55%). The next columns present the information separately for males and females. Considering the occurrence by gender, 53% of the males and 68% of the females reported that they had something thrown at them. Chi-square analysis ($\chi 2 = 11.9$, df = 4)

Table 9
Rate of Physical Abuse[a]

Abuse		n	%
Physical Abuse at Home			
Total	(N = 176)	142	81
Males	(N = 107)	85	79
Females	(N = 69)	57	83
Physical Abuse on the Street			
Total	(N = 176)	114	65
Males	(N = 107)	72	67
Female	(N = 69)	42	61

a. Abuse is defined as Severe or Very Severe Violence acts.

indicated that the proportion of females who experienced this type of behavior is significantly higher that the proportion of males. Females also experienced more incidents when food or clothing were denied to them and had more injuries that resulted in difficulty walking or sitting.

It is surprising how much violence this group of adolescents has experienced. A 17 year old male tells of watching his younger brother being abused and having vague memories and dreams of being burned and other abuses by his foster family. Another runaway said, "It doesn't hurt anymore, when you're a punching bag you can't feel anything." A runaway reported being disciplined (hit) with a stick that had nails sticking out of it. One runaway recalled, "It must have happened a million times, everyday, all the time, from the day I met him (stepfather) to the day I ran away. A 16 year old described high levels of violent experiences and explains that she cannot remember more than the past five years. However, her sisters told her that she had her hand burned on the stove and had her arm broken when she was younger. She considered this to be normal discipline.

Several of the runaways suggested reasons for the abuse they had experienced. Among the reasons were: (a) normal discipline, (b) parental characteristic or background, and (c) their own behavior. Runaways talked about parents who abused because of drinking, bad tempers, or going through a tough time. A runaway suggested that the

Table 10
Physical Abuse at Home by Category of Violence[a]

Behaviors	Total (n = 195)	Male (n = 118)	Female (n = 77)
A. Minor Violence Acts			
1. Threw something*	58	53	68
2. Grabbed/thrown around	55	49	64
3. Denied food/clothes	40	42	36
4. Denied school/medical*	17	13	25
5. Pulled muscle from fight	27	23	30
B. Severe Violence Acts[b]			
6. Repeatedly slapped	50	43	60
7. Hit with object that left: Mark/bruise/cut/welt	56	47	70
8. Tied up/rope burns	7	5	6
9. Injured had difficulty walking/sitting*	42	34	55
10. Threatened with gun/weapon	30	25	38
C. Very Severe Violence Acts[b]			
11. Kicked	47	43	53
12. Beat up/punched	56	55	58
13. Assaulted/gun or weapon	13	11	16
14. Head banged	41	37	47
15. Burned/scalded	12	9	17
16. Held under water	6	6	6
17. Injured-Hospital	13	9	19

* Significant differences between males and females at .05.
a. Percentage rounded to nearest whole percent.
b. Abuse is defined as Severe or Very Severe Violence.

abuse he experienced was a result of his own involvement with drugs. However, one runaway who blamed himself for the violence he had experienced at home, reported being very severely abused by the age of three. I wonder what a three year old child could do that would justify the use of very severe violence.

Table 11

Age of Onset of Physical Abuse at Home[a]

Age	Total n	%	Male n	%	Female n	%
Early Childhood (6 or younger)	64	45	35	42	29	49
Childhood (7 - 11)	47	33	29	35	18	31
Early Adolescence (12 -15)	23	16	12	14	11	19
Adolescence (16 - 20)	9	6	8	10	1	2
Total	143	81	84	79	59	86

Note. Missing data and rounding may result in apparent inconsistencies.

a. Percentage of respondents rounded to nearest whole percent.

Age of Onset. Table 11 presents information about age of onset of physical abuse at home. Age of onset is displayed for the total group and for males and females separately. Ages are collapsed into four categories: early childhood, ages 0 - 6; childhood, ages 7 - 11; early adolescence, ages 12 - 15; and adolescence, ages 16 - 20. For those reporting physical abuse at home, just under half of the runaways report the abuse beginning in early childhood. Considering both childhood categories together, the risk of onset of abuse in childhood is 77% for males and 79% for females. The risk of onset of abuse decreases in adolescence; however 10% of the males who reported experiencing physical abuse indicated that the first occurrence was after the age of 16. The median age of onset for physical abuse at home was 8 years of age.

Frequency of Physical Abuse at Home. The frequency of abusive incidents at home is presented in Table 12. The majority of those abused (84%) were abused very frequently (53%). Very frequent occurrence is defined as 50 or more times, while frequent occurrence is between 10 and 49 times. Infrequent occurrence is defined as

Table 12
Frequency of Physical Abuse at Home[a]

Frequency	Total n	Total %	Male n	Male %	Female n	Female %
Rare (1-2)	25	17	18	21	7	12
Infrequent (3-9)	14	10	9	10	5	8
Frequent (10-49)	30	20	14	16	16	26
Very Frequent (50+)	79	53	46	53	33	54
Total	148	84	87	81	61	88

a. Percentage rounded to nearest whole percent.

between 3 and 9 instances and rare occurrence is 1 or 2 times. Males (21%) report rare instances of abuse more often than females (12%).

Severity of Physical Abuse at Home. Table 13 lists the specific acts and the categories of severity of physical abuse. However, abusive incidents may involve more than one type of behavior. Severity of abuse reflects the most severe type of behavior reported by the adolescent. For example, many of the runaways who report having experienced minor acts of violence also report having experienced more severe forms of violence. Thus, they would be included in the Severe category rather than the Minor category. Table 13 presents the information on severity of abuse. Only 3% of the sample report Minor abuse. Over 95% of the abused runaways report being victims of seriously abusive behaviors. The Very Severe category refers to behaviors such as kicking, punching, burning, and tying with a rope. These are the assaults that over 80% of the runaways experienced in their homes. It is amazing that only 50% of the runaways cited physical abuse as an important reason for leaving home.

Physical Abuse on the Street

Table 14 summarizes the experiences reported by the runaways concerning physical abuse on the street by specific behaviors and categories of violence. An overall reduction in the percentage of runaways reporting being victims of specific violent acts can be observed. For example, 55% of the sample had been grabbed and

Table 13
Severity of Physical Abuse at Home

Severity	Total Sample (n = 176) n	%	Male (n = 107) n	%	Female (n = 69) n	%
Minor	6	3	2	2	4	6
Severe	18	10	12	11	6	9
Very Severe	124	70	73	68	51	74
Total Abused	142	81	85	79	57	83

a. Abuse is defined as Severe and Very Severe violence.

thrown around while living at home, but only 27% experienced this form of abuse while on the streets. The two categories that increased while on the street were being threatened (home = 30%, street = 51%) and assaulted (home = 13%, street = 27%) with a gun or weapon. An examination of relationship of specific violent experiences and gender indicates that the pattern of slight increase of risk for females at home seems to be partially reversed on the street. Males are at a significantly higher risk for being threatened (58% vs. 42%) and being assaulted (33% vs. 18%) with a gun or weapon. On the other hand, significantly more females (31%) experience being repeatedly slapped than males (13%). Figures 1 through 3 graphically present the comparison of the specific types of abuse experienced by the runaways at home and on the street.

One runaway, who had experienced a great deal of violence on the street, told the interviewer that the pimps or jealous hookers were responsible for the abuse. She thought it was because she refused to "have a pimp of my own". Several runaways, who described a lot of violence "on the street" were actually abused while married, but the marriage was part of the runaway episode. One explained, "He was drunk a lot and he couldn't control his temper, even when sober." Another said, "I deserved it. He would want me to shut up and I didn't. So I got hit." Several males, who experienced much violence on the street, did not consider themselves abused; they were just fighting. One runaway said, "On the street violence is life."

Table 14
Physical Abuse on the Street by Category of Violence[a]

Behaviors	Total (n = 195)	Male (n = 118)	Female (n = 77)
A. Minor Violence Acts			
1. Threw something	30	30	30
2. Grabbed/thrown around	27	23	32
3. Denied food/clothes	8	9	5
4. Denied school/medical	7	8	5
5. Pulled muscle from fight	27	28	25
B. Severe Violence Acts[b]			
6. Repeatedly slapped*	20	13	31
7. Hit with object that left:			
Mark/bruise/cut/welt	23	23	21
8. Tied up/rope burns	7	6	8
9. Injured had difficulty			
walking/sitting	17	15	19
10. Threatened with gun/weapon*	51	58	42
C. Very Severe Violence Acts[b]			
11. Kicked	38	40	35
12. Beat up/punched	56	58	53
13. Assaulted/gun or weapon*	27	33	18
14. Head banged	27	25	30
15. Burned/scalded	12	14	17
16. Held under water	3	4	1
17. Injured-Hospital	12	9	16

* Significant differences between males and females at .05.
a. Percentage rounded to nearest whole percent.
b. Defined as abuse.

Figures 4 through 6 graphically display the comparison of the percentage of runaways experiencing specific types of violence at home and on the street. The figures dramatically demonstrate that, for most types of violence, the street is a haven of relative safety when compared to the abuse suffered at home by the runaways.

Figure 4
Minor Physical Violence

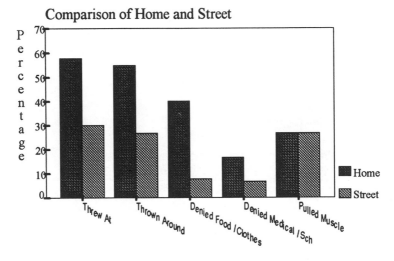

Figure 5
Severe Physical Violence

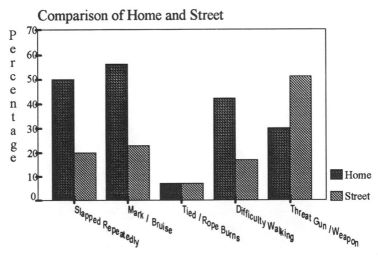

Figure 6
Very Severe Physical Violence

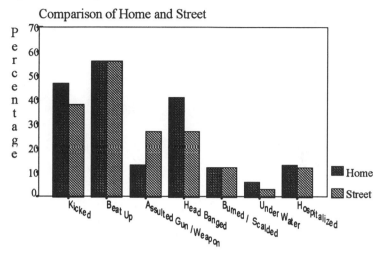

Comparison of Home and Street

Age of Onset of Physical Abuse on the Street. Age of onset of physical abuse on the street is presented in Table 15. Although most (82%) of the abused runaways were first abused on the street sometime during adolescence (age 12 and older), approximately 24% of the males and 7% of the females were abused on the street before the age of 12.

Frequency of Physical Abuse on the Street. Table 16 displays the frequency of physical abuse on the street. Approximately 65% of the runaways report being abused on the streets. In contrast to physical abuse at home, physical abuse on the street was usually a rare occurrence (33%), especially for females (43%). About 30% of the runaways who experienced abuse on the street reported that they were abused very frequently. This is equivalent to 19% of the total sample. The reduction in the frequency of physical abuse on the street could be because the runaway is able to avoid the perpetrator of the abuse, which is difficult while living at home with the perpetrator. However, the reduction is frequency of abuse might also be attributed to the reduced amount of time living on the street versus living at home.

Table 15
Age of Onset of Physical Abuse on the Street[a]

Age	Total		Male		Female	
	n	%	n	%	n	%
Early Childhood (6 or younger)	5	5	4	6	1	2
Childhood (7 - 11)	14	13	12	18	2	5
Early Adolescence (12 -15)	43	40	22	33	21	52
Adolescence (16 - 20)	46	43	29	43	17	42
Total	108	61	67	63	41	59

Note. Missing data and rounding may result in apparent inconsistencies.
a. Percentage of rounded to nearest whole percent.

Table 16
Frequency of Physical Abuse on the Street[a]

Frequency	Total		Male		Female	
	n	%	n	%	n	%
Rare (1-2)	38	33	20	27	18	43
Infrequent (3-9)	18	16	12	16	6	14
Frequent (10-49)	25	22	20	27	5	12
Very Frequent (50+)	34	30	21	29	13	31
Total	115	65	73	68	42	61

a. Percentage rounded to nearest whole percent.

Severity of Physical Abuse on the Street. Information about the severity of physical abuse on the street is displayed in Table 17. Over half of the runaways report experiencing very severe physical abuse on the street. Of the 114 runaways who were abused on the street, over

90% (n = 104) report the abuse to be very severe. Figure 7 graphically displays the comparison of severity of physical abuse at home and on the street.

Table 17
Severity of Physical Abuse on the Street[a]

Severity	Total Sample (n = 176)		Male (n = 107)		Female (n = 69)	
	n	%	n	%	n	%
Minor	1	1	1	1	0	0
Severe	10	6	5	7	5	7
Very Severe	104	59	67	92	37	54
Total Abused[b]	114	65	72	67	42	61

a. Percentage rounded to nearest whole percent.
b. Abuse defined as Severe and Very Severe violence.

Figure 7
Severity of Physical Abuse at Home and on the Street

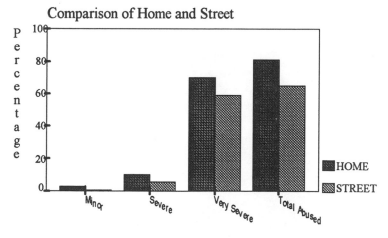

Note: Total abused = Severe and Very Severe.

The runaways in this study experienced high rates of physical abuse at home prior to running away (81%). However only 50% of the runaways indicated that the abuse they suffered at home was a major reason for leaving home. They cited difficulty in getting along with the male and female caretakers and feeling unloved as important reasons for leaving. This suggests that the psychological aspects of living in a dysfunctional family had more negative consequences than the actual physical abuse aspects.

While life on the street was accompanied by a significant amount of physical abuse, the percentage of runaways experiencing the abuse and the severity of abuse decreased on the street. For this sample of runaways, the street is a relative haven of safety when compared to the home.

VI
Sexual Abuse of Runaways

This study examined the sexual abuse history of runaway adolescents. Participants were asked specific behaviorally-oriented questions about their sexual background. The section of the interview that addressed sexual abuse was specifically placed at the end of the interview. Typically the adolescent and the interviewer had been working together for approximately an hour before this sensitive section was attempted.

The sexual history inquired into multiple areas. We asked how the subjects first learned about sex. We asked them about having sex: (a) the first time, (b) with a family member, or (c) with an authority figure. The youths were asked if they had been in sexual situations when there was violence or threat of violence. They were asked if anyone had ever wanted to take pictures of them in the nude or while having sex, if anyone had offered them money for sex, or if they had been involved in hustling or prostitution.

SEXUAL ABUSE

Sexual experiences were coded as abusive if it met one of the characteristics of sexually abusive behavior:[1]

1. report of the presence of force, threat, or coercion;
2. age discrepancy (five years for subjects younger than 14, 10 years for subjects 14 or older);
3. age inappropriateness of experience (cunnilingus, anilingus, intercourse, and sodomy before the age of 14); or
4. presence of illegal activity, such as prostitution or pornography.

Early Sexual Experience

Learning About Sex. The youth were asked to describe how they learned about sex. The responses were coded for evidence of abuse. Using the preceding criteria, 12% of the 195 respondents first learned about sex in a abusive experience, with 5% of the males and 22% of the females reporting abusive introductions to sex..

One female reported that she was molested by a babysitter when she was 2 years old. She does not actually remember this but indicated that her parents told her. One youth reported that her "foster dad" sexually abused her for 2 years from the ages of 5 to 7. She reports that the memory is "vague, unclear, blocked" but that she remembers needing to go the hospital for stitches.

First Sexual Experience. In describing their first sexual experience, 29% of the sample reported experiences that met the criteria of abuse; of these 16% were males and 49% were females. For some of the youth their first sexual experiences was how they learned about sex. For example, a female reported that she learned about sex when she was raped. One of the female adolescents described her first sexual experience as "My father was drunk, he lay down on my bed and started to feel me up. I told him I needed to go to the washroom. I got my mother and she took him to his own bed."

The overall rate of early sexually is 31%, that is 60 of the 195 runaways reported abusive first learning about sex or first sexual experiences. Age of first sexual experience is reported in Table 18.

Table 18

Age of First Sexual Experience[a]

Age	Total (n = 194)	Male (n = 117)	Female (n = 77)
0 -5	9	7	13
6 - 10	22	20	25
11 - 13	26	32	17
14 - 20	43	41	44

a. Percentage rounded to nearest whole percent.

Sex with Family Member

The runaways were asked if they had ever had a sexual experience with a member of their families. Of the 194 adolescents responding, 38% responded positively (30% of the males and 50% of the females). Table 19 presents information about the identity of the family member with whom the runaway reported sexual experiences. The experience was defined as abusive when the family member was an adult. Overall, 8% of the sample had abusive sexual experiences with a family member.

Table 19
Identity of Family Member[a]

Relationship	Total (n = 74)	Male (n = 37)	Female (n = 37)
Father	10	3	17
Step-father	5	0	11
Mother	3	5	0
Brother	8	8	8
Sister	10	14	5

a. Percentage rounded to nearest whole percent.

Unwanted Sex with an Authority Figure

Twenty-four percent of the sample reported having unwanted sexual experiences with authority figures, 21% of the males and 24% of the females. Two females reported that they had to have sex with their bosses at a strip bar in order to get paid. A male indicated that he had sex with his teacher to get better grades.

Sex and Violence

Although the youths had already described many abusive sexual experiences, we asked them, "Have you ever been in any situation where there was violence or threat of violence, where you were afraid of being sexually assaulted, other than the time you have already mentioned? Sixteen percent of the runways (9% males and 16% females) reported additional abusive experiences where violence was a factor.

A female reported that in three different sexual relationships, she had been forced to have sex at times when she tried to refuse. One female who had been sexually abused as a youngster, reported that on several occasions, men she was dating would insist on sex. She just "gave in and did it like a robot." One runway recalled an incident when a stranger followed her from a mall, pulled her into some bushes and raped her. She never pressed charges. One of the youths reported that a "John" once forced her to do things she did not want. He said, "You're just a whore; no one will miss you."

Rape

Many of the previous situations involved rape; however, we asked the runaways if, other than the situations already discussed, they had ever been raped. Surprisingly, an additional 24% of the sample responded "Yes", 13% of the males and 38% of the females.

One runaway explained that her best friend's boyfriend raped her when she slept over at her friend's house. Another female reported being a victim of rape by her uncle, but she became upset and did not want to discuss the incident. One female described being gang-raped by four strangers.

Pornography and Prostitution

Thirty-two percent of the sample (31% of the males and 35% of the females) responded positively when asked if anyone had ever asked to take pictures of them in the nude or while having sex for money. One female reported that a man exposed himself to her and offered her $60 for sex. She refused. Another female needed food and a place to stay. She could not get a job. She met a pimp and he charmed her into prostitution. Another runaway was talked into "walking the streets" by her boyfriend so that they could get money and buy a little house. She felt betrayed, because she thought he loved her.

Overall Rate of Sexual Abuse

The percent of the runaways who responded positively to one of the sexually abusive situations was 71%, which included 50% of the males and 86% of the females. Of those sexually abused, a caretaker is the most frequently cited perpetrator of the abuse; 84% of the sexually abused females and 46% of the sexually abused males report a caretaker as the perpetrator.

Age of Onset of Sexual Abuse

Age of onset of sexual abuse is presented in Table 20. Eighteen percent of the sexually abused in the runaway sample reported being victimized before the age of seven and 29% of the males and 41% of the females reported onset of sexual abuse before age 12. The majority (55%) of the sexually abused males reported the onset of the abuse to be after age 16, while only 27% of the females reported onset after age 16. Thus, sexual abuse in females was often unrelated to sexual maturity.

Frequency of Sexual Abuse

Frequency of sexual abuse is displayed in Table 21. Over one-half of the sexually abused runaways reported the occurrence to be either rare or infrequent. Twenty-seven percent of the females reported the abuse to be very frequent, while only 16% of the males reported very frequent sexual abuse.

Table 20

Age of Onset of Sexual Abuse

Age	Total		Male		Female	
	n	%	n	%	n	%
Early Childhood (6 or younger)	16	18	7	18	9	18
Childhood (7 - 11)	16	18	4	11	12	24
Early Adolescence (12 -15)	22	25	6	16	16	31
Adolescence (16 - 20)	35	40	21	55	14	27
Total	89	51	38	36	51	74

Note. Missing data and rounding may result in apparent inconsistencies.

a. Percentage of respondents rounded to nearest whole percent.

Table 21
Frequency of Sexual Abuse[a]

Frequency	Total n	%	Male n	%	Female n	%
Rare (1-2)	37	29	21	28	16	29
Infrequent (3-9)	43	33	24	32	19	34
Frequent (10-49)	23	18	17	23	6	11
Very Frequent (50+)	27	21	12	16	15	27
Total	130	74	74	69	56	81

a. Percentage rounded to nearest whole percent.

Severity of Sexual Abuse

The severity of the experience was defined by Russell's three categories of severity of abuse.[2]

Russell's Severity Scale:
1. Russell 1 (Least Severe-Body Violation) is defined as completed or attempted acts of intentional touching of buttocks, thigh, leg, or other body part, clothed breasts or genitals, or kissing; forced or unforced.
2. Russell 2 (Severe-Genital Violation) is defined as completed or attempted genital fondling, simulated intercourse, or digital penetration; both forced and unforced.
3. Russell 3 (Most Severe-Penetration) is defined as completed or attempted vaginal, oral, or anal intercourse, cunnilingus, or anilingus; forced or unforced.

Table 22 presents the information on severity of sexual abuse by specific type of abuse. Twenty-five percent of those who report being abused by a family member indicated that the experience involved touching of the body (Russell 1); 39% report genital touching (Russell 2); and 37% report genital penetration (Russell 3). It is interesting that just under half of the rape incidents involve non-penetration.

Table 22
Severity of Sexual Abuse[a]

Type	n	Russell 1	Russell 2	Russell 3
Family	40	25	39	37
Authority	43	42	19	40
Violence	32	44	25	31
Rape	44	14	23	61

a. Percentage rounded to nearest whole percent.

NOTES

1. Janus, M., Archambault, F.X., & Welsh, L.A. (1988). Physical and sexual abuse in runaway homeless youth. Paper presented at the 96th annual meeting of the American Psychological Association, Atlanta, GA.

2. Russell, DE. (1984). Sexual exploitation: Rape. Child sexual abuse and workplace harassment. Newbury Park, CA: Sage Publications, Inc.

VII
Self-Esteem Among Runaways

Runaway youths are a special population of adolescents who have abandoned their homes and family environments. Therefore, by definition, runaways perceive their families to be unable to meet their needs. This chapter will present information on the relationships among self-esteem and physical abuse at home, physical abuse on the street, and sexual abuse of adolescent runaways. Specific characteristics of abuse, such as age of onset, severity, and frequency, will be examined

Table 23 displays means and standard deviations of the Rosenberg Self-Esteem Inventory (RSE) for both the runaway and high school samples. The average RSE for runaways is 2.94, while the average RSE for high school students is 3.15. The average self-esteem reported by females is lower than that reported by the males in both the runaway and high school sample.

Table 23
Self-Esteem in Runaway and High School Sample

Sample	n	Mean	SD
Runaways			
Total	167	2.94	.55
Male	101	2.99	.55
Female	66	2.87	.54
High School			
Total	173	3.15	.45
Male	83	3.25	.43
Female	89	3.05	.44

THEORETICAL MODEL

Runaways are adolescents who, as a group, have typically experienced high levels of physical abuse at home, physical abuse on the streets, and sexual abuse. How much of the variation in self-esteem of adolescent runaways can be explained by these variables? We developed a theoretical model that was comprised of the three abuse factors (physical abuse at home, physical abuse on the street, and sexual abuse) which were hypothesized to cause the self-esteem factor. The specific characteristics of abuse, such as age of onset, frequency, and severity were identified as indicators of the latent abuse factors. Responses to the Rosenberg Self-Esteem Inventory were identified as indicators of the latent self-esteem factor. Figure 3 (Chapter 4) displays the predicted relationships among the factors and indicators.

Relationships Among the Latent Factors

This section describes the results of the analyses addressing the first research question: Can the self-esteem of adolescent runaways be explained by the theoretical model of inter-relationships among the abuse factors?

The correlations among the latent abuse factors are presented in Table 24. The square of the correlation (R^2) is the percent of variation in one factor which can be explained or predicted by the other factor. For example, only approximately 5% of the variation in characteristics of physical abuse on the street can be explained or predicted by the characteristics of physical abuse at home. On the other hand, 25% of the characteristics of sexual abuse can be predicted by the characteristics of physical abuse at home.

Table 25 displays the correlations among the abuse factors and self-esteem. The data did not support the hypothesis that the characteristics of abuse experienced by the runaways could predict their self-esteem. Thus, self-esteem in adolescent runaways cannot be predicted by the specific characteristics (age of onset, frequency, and severity) of abuse suffered either at home or on the street.

The model was tested to determine if the patterns of inter-relationships were the same for males and females. No significant differences were found in the theoretical model for males and females. Thus, the absence of a relationship between self-esteem and physical abuse at home, physical abuse on the street, or sexual abuse is observed in both males and females.

Table 24
Relationships Among the Abuse Factors

Factors	Correlation	R^2
Physical Abuse at Home and on the Street	.23	.05
Physical Abuse at Home and Sexual Abuse	.51	.26
Physical Abuse on the Street and Sexual Abuse	.36	.13

Table 25
Correlations Among Abuse and Self-Esteem

Factor	Correlation	R^2
Self-Esteem and		
Physical Abuse at Home	.01	.00
Physical Abuse on the Street	.00	.00
Sexual Abuse	.11	.01

COMPARISON BETWEEN RUNAWAYS AND NON-RUNAWAYS

We compared high school students' and runaways' responses to the Rosenberg Self-Esteem Inventory to determine if, as a group, runaways differed from high school students with respect to level of self-esteem. This question was extended to determine if differences in self-esteem were observed between males and females and if any interaction existed between gender and group (high school and runaway).

Table 26 presents the results of the two-way analysis of variance used to determine if there were differences in self-esteem between the high school and runaway adolescents. The significant F (17.40) for Group indicates that the observed differences between high school students' (mean = 3.15) and runaways' (mean = 2.94) self-esteem were significant (means are reported in Table 20). High school students typically exhibited a higher self-esteem than runaways.

This result was consistent with the literature and may explain why specific characteristics of abuse were unable to predict self-esteem in the runaway population, for by definition, the runaways have escaped an intolerable home situation regardless of the specific characteristics of the antecedents. Table 26 also reveals gender differences in self-esteem. The significant difference between males and females is supported by the literature. The absence of interaction between gender and group indicates that the differences in self-esteem between males and females occurs in both the runaway and high school sample.

Thus, runaways typically exhibit lower self-esteem than their high school peers and regardless of group (high school or runaway), females exhibit lower self-esteem than males.

Table 26

Analysis of Variance of Self-Esteem in Runaways and High School Students

Source	SS	DF	MS	F
Main Effects				
Group (Runaways / High School)	4.21	1	4.21	17.40**
Gender	2.16	1	2.16	8.91**
Interaction				
Group X Gender	.11	1	.11	.44
Residual	81.06	335	.24	
Total	86.88	338	.25	

* $p < .05$
** $p < .01$

SELF-ESTEEM OF RUNAWAYS

Types of Abuse. We examined the question: Are there differences in self-esteem of males and females among the types of abuse (physical, sexual, both physical and sexual, and none) of runaway adolescents? This question compared four groups of adolescent runaways to determine if self-esteem was related to (a) group membership (physically abused, sexually abused, both physically and sexually abused, and no abuse) or (b) gender.

Table 27 presents results of the two-way analysis of variance addressing the question. The analysis tested three null hypotheses: (a) there are no significant differences between types of abuse with respect to self-esteem of adolescent runaways, (b) there are no significant differences between male and female adolescent runaways with respect to self-esteem, and (c) there is no significant interaction between type of abuse and gender of adolescent runaways with respect to self-esteem. The nonsignificant F's for each of these hypotheses indicated that there were no differences between these groups. Thus, self-esteem in adolescent runaways is not related to the type of abuse they have experienced in their lives.

Table 27

Analysis of Variance of Self-Esteem by Type of Abuse and Gender

Source	SS	DF	MS	F
Main Effects				
Type[a]	.61	3	.20	.67
Gender	.54	1	.54	1.80
Interaction				
Type X Gender	.39	3	.13	.43
Residual	47.98	159	.30	
Total	49.59	166	.30	

a. Type of abuse = physical; sexual; physical and sexual; and no abuse.

Frequency of Abuse

Self-esteem data were examined to determine if differences exist between adolescent runaways who had experienced no abuse, rare abuse (1 or 2 occurrences), and multiple occurrences of abuse. Separate analyses were performed for frequency of physical abuse at home, physical abuse on the street, and sexual abuse.

Physical Abuse at Home. Table 28 presents the results of analysis of variance examining differences between frequency of abuse (none, rare, or multiple) at home with respect to adolescent runaways' self-esteem. As seen in the table, although there are no significant main effects, the interaction between gender and frequency of abuse is significant. The graph of the interaction (see Figure 8) displays the results of this analysis. A curvilinear relationship between self-esteem and frequency of physical abuse at home was exhibited for both males and females. The literature suggests that males exhibit higher self-esteem than females. This pattern was observed in this study for adolescent runaway males who experienced no abuse or multiple occurrence of abuse. However, males who experienced rare occurrences of physical abuse at home demonstrated lower self-esteem than females. Alternatively, adolescent female runaways exhibited lower self-esteem than male runaways except when physical abuse at home was rare.

Table 28

Analysis of Variance of Self-Esteem by Frequency of Physical Abuse at Home and Gender

Source	SS	DF	MS	F
Main Effects				
Frequency of Occurrence[a]	.09	2	.04	.21
Gender	.15	1	.15	.51.
Interaction				
Frequency X Gender	2.20	2	1.10	3.84*
Residual	46.17	161	.29	
Total	49.59	166	.30	

* $p < .05$
a. Frequency = none, rare (1 - 2 times), and multiple.

Figure 8
Interaction Between Gender and Frequency of Physical Abuse at Home With Respect to Self-Esteem

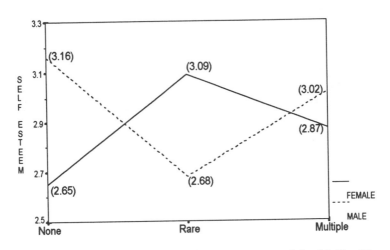

Note. SD = .55. Cells have unequal numbers: None (M = 18, F = 8), Rare (M = 16, F = 7), and Multiple (M = 67, F = 51).

On the Street. Table 29 presents the results of the ANOVA examining differences between frequency of physical abuse on the street for both males and females with respect to self-esteem. None of the three null hypotheses was rejected; thus, there was no difference between frequency (none, rare, and multiple occurrences) of physical abuse on the street, between males and females and no interaction between frequency of abuse on the street and gender with respect to self-esteem of adolescent runaways.

Sexual Abuse. Table 30 presents results of the analysis of variance examining differences between gender and frequency of sexual abuse with respect to self-esteem. Neither gender nor frequency exhibited significant differences. However, the interaction of frequency of sexual abuse and gender on self-esteem is significant. As can be seen in Figure 9, the curvilinear relationship between frequency of sexual abuse and self-esteem for both males and females is similar to that observed for physical abuse at home. Runaway adolescent males had higher self-esteem except when they were victims of rare

Table 29
Analysis of Variance of Self-Esteem by Frequency of Physical Abuse on the Street and Gender

Source	SS	DF	MS	F
Main Effects				
Frequency of Occurrence[a]	.75	2	.38	1.27
Gender	.49	1	.49	1.66
Interaction				
Frequency X Gender	.53	2	.26	.89
Residual	47.75	161	.30	
Total	49.59	166	.30	

a. Frequency = none, rare (1 - 2 times), and multiple.

Table 30
Analysis of Variance of Self-Esteem by Frequency of Sexual Abuse and Gender

Source	SS	DF	MS	F
Main Effects				
Frequency of Occurrence[a]	1.28	2	.64	2.34
Gender	.16	1	.16	.57
Interaction				
Frequency X Gender	4.53	2	2.26	8.29*
Residual	47.75	161	.30	
Total	49.59	166	.30	

* $p < .05$
a. Frequency = none, rare (1 - 2 times), and multiple.

occurrences of sexual abuse. Females, on the other hand, exhibited lower self-esteem except when sexual abuse was a rare occurrence. It should be noted that the number of cases in some of the

Figure 9
Interaction Between Gender and Frequency of Sexual
Abuse With Respect to Self-Esteem

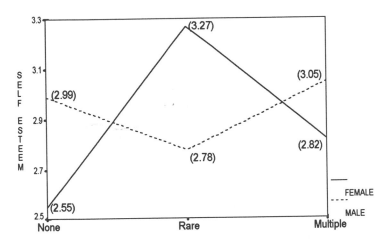

Note. SD = .55. Cells have unequal numbers: None (M = 31, F = 13),
Rare (M = 20, F = 15), and Multiple (M = 50, F = 38).

categories was small; therefore, these estimates may be unstable and
caution is suggested when interpreting these findings.

The self-esteem of runaways is significantly lower than that of a
sample of high school students. Analyses of specific abuse-related
characteristics of the runaways could not explain the variation in self-
esteem. In this sample of adolescent runaways, self-esteem was not
related to frequency, severity, or age of onset of physical abuse at
home, physical abuse on the street, or sexual abuse. The female
runaways reported lower self-esteem than the males, which is
consistent with findings in the general population. However, different
patterns emerged for males and females when examining frequency of
abuse and self-esteem. Under the circumstances of rare occurrences of
physical abuse at home or sexual abuse, males reported lower self-
esteem than females.

VIII
Conclusions

PHYSICAL ABUSE

Runaways interviewed for this study exhibited a high rate of abuse. Physical abuse is defined as experiencing severely violent actions, such as being repeatedly slapped, hit with an object that left a welt, bruise or mark, tied up, kicked, or beaten. Table 10 (see Chapter 5) displays the entire list of behaviors that are defined as abusive. The rate of physical abuse among runaways in this study (81%) is similar to rates found for runaways by Farber and Kinast[1] and Houghten and Golembiewski.[2] This rate is much higher than the estimated rate of 9.1% for the general population.[3] Although the rate of physical abuse on the street for runaways was previously unreported, the high rate of crime and violence on the street would lend credence to the 65% rate found in the present research. What is surprising is the lower rate of physical violence suffered on the street than at home (81%) by this runaway sample. For this population, the notion of the street as a place of violence is overshadowed by the violence experienced in the home.

Physical Abuse at Home

Physical abuse at home typically begins at an early age for both males and females. Almost half (49%) of the females experienced the onset of physical abuse at home before the age of seven, while 42% of the males were physically abused before that age. This finding supports previous research which concluded that physical abuse occurs quite frequently to very young children.[4] Over half of the abused male and female runaways reported very frequent (50 or more episodes) of physical abuse in the home. Of the remaining cases, more males (21%) reported rare or infrequent (10%) instances of such abuse, while more females (26%) reported frequent episodes. The overwhelming majority of both male and female runaways (84%) described the abuse suffered as severe. Although the high rate of unreported perpetrators of abuse prevented statistical consideration of this variable, those who identified the perpetrator indicated almost exclusively that it was a parent or caretaker (96%). Thus, physical abuse at home begins young, occurs frequently, is severe and is committed by a parent or parent-substitute for the typical runaway adolescent.

The findings of this study differ from the existing literature in several ways. Previous research indicates that although very young children are at risk of physical abuse, the risk increases again for adolescents.[5] The pattern of risk reported in this study demonstrated decreasing risk of physical abuse at home with increasing age. This decrease in risk of physical abuse at home during adolescence may be explained by the runaway episode itself which removes the adolescent from the home. Previous research indicates that males are at higher risk of physical abuse than females.[6] In this study females demonstrated higher risk and higher frequency of physical abuse at home. Previous research also indicates males suffer more severe abuse than females.[7] However, this study found no gender difference. Thus, the runaway population seems to differ from the general population in several respects.

Physical Abuse on the Street

Physical abuse on the street did not occur until late adolescence for 43% of the runaway sample, although a surprising 24% of the males had experienced abuse on the street before the age of 12; for females this figure was only 7%. In contrast to physical abuse at home, only 30% of the abused runaways report very frequent physical abuse on the street. Many females (43%) report that physical abuse on the street is a rare event, while physical abuse of males may be either rare or infrequent. Over 90% of the abused runaways reported the abuse to be severe; and, females (88%) reported only a slightly lower rate than males (92%). Thus, in contrast to physical abuse at home, physical abuse on the street typically begins after age 15 and the occurrence is rare (1 to 2 episodes), especially for females.

When looking at the combination of physical abuse at home and on the street, the pattern of very young risk and adolescent risk that emerged in previous studies is supported in this study.[8] Like physical abuse at home, physical abuse on the street, when it occurs, tends to be severe.

SEXUAL ABUSE

Older adolescent onset (16 to 20) is typical for sexually abused males (55%), while sexual abuse of females (41%) is apt to occur before adolescence (12 or younger). Sexual abuse is more apt to be rare or infrequent than physical abuse, although 27% of the sexually abused females reported very frequent abuse. Less than half of the sexually abused males (43%) reported severe abuse (i.e., penetration), while over half the abused females (59%) reported penetration. The caretaker is the most commonly cited perpetrator for female sexual abuse (84%), while males cited caretakers (46%) and others (55%) at almost equal rates. Thus, sexual abuse does not have the same profile for males and females. More runaway females reported sexual abuse and reported it occurring before adolescence. Very frequent occurrence and penetration were more apt to occur to females than males. Males experienced non-caretakers committing sexual abuse more frequently than did females.

The results of this study differ from Russell, who reported the highest risk of sexual abuse to be between the ages of 10 and 14 for females.[9] The work of Finkelhor suggests that the age of greatest risk for both males and females is between 10 and 12 years, although boys have been shown to have an increased risk of abuse at a very young age.[10] Previous information regarding frequency of abuse is consistent with the results of this study. Approximately 30% of the victims report very frequent abuse and about half report single or rare occurrences.[11]

SELF-ESTEEM

Theoretical Model

Analysis of the theoretical model failed to confirm the hypothesized relationship between the abuse factors and self-esteem in the runaway adolescent. Although the results suggest the model provides a satisfactory method of measuring abuse, it is not useful in explaining the variation in self-esteem in this sample of runaway adolescents.

Previous research has indicated lowered self-esteem as a result of physical abuse[12] and sexual abuse.[13] However, these studies did not include runaway adolescents. Perhaps the absence of a significant relationship between the types of abuse measured in this study and self-esteem is attributable to other variables that are associated with running away. Runaway youths are a special population of adolescents who have abandoned their homes and family environments. Therefore, by definition, runaways perceive their families to be unable to meet their needs. It could be hypothesized that factors important enough to precipitate running away also would influence self-esteem. Psychological maltreatment, verbal aggression, and neglect have been associated with dysfunctional families and related to lowered self-esteem.[14] Only 40% of the sample cited physical or sexual abuse as important reasons for running away, while almost 60% cited difficulty with relationships and feeling unloved as important reasons. The inclusion of these variables in future research might help to clarify the relationship between abuse and self-esteem for runaways.

Comparison of Runaways and High School Students

Analysis of variance between high school students and runaways with respect to self-esteem demonstrated significantly higher self-esteem in the high school population. There was no interaction between group (high school and runaway) and gender, which indicates that the pattern of relationships among the variables is the same for males and females.

This result is consistent with the literature. Special populations, such as runaways,[15] physically abused,[16] and sexually abused[17] have exhibited lowered self-esteem. Thus, even though within the runaway group level of abuse was not related to self-esteem, significant differences in self-esteem existed between the runaway and non-runaway groups.

Types of Abuse

Results demonstrated no significant difference in self-esteem regardless of the type of abuse suffered. The interaction between type of abuse and gender with respect to self-esteem was also not significant, indicating that the pattern of differences is the same for males and females. These results are consistent with the earlier analysis of the theoretical model. Within this population of runaways, self-esteem cannot be explained by the factors of physical or sexual abuse. Again, other factors, such as verbal abuse or dysfunctional family that were not measured in this study may explain the apparent lack of relationship between demonstrated abuse and self-esteem.

Frequency of Abuse

No significant differences in self-esteem were observed for different levels of frequency of abuse (no abuse, rare, and frequent); however, significant interactions emerged between gender and frequency of occurrence of physical abuse at home and sexual abuse, but not physical abuse on the street. A curvilinear relationship was observed for both males and females. These interactions demonstrated higher levels of self-esteem for runaway males except when the occurrences of physical abuse at home and sexual abuse were rare. These findings are somewhat consistent with the literature that suggest males have higher self-esteem than females. However, when physical abuse at home or sexual abuse is experienced infrequently, the effect on self-esteem was reversed with males exhibiting lower self-esteem than females. It appears that when the youth are either abused or not abused consistently, the effect on self-esteem is different from when the abuse is an unusual event. Perhaps it is the unpredictable nature of the rare occurrence that accounts for the different effect on self-esteem. However, these results must be viewed as preliminary because the small number of cases in some of the groups may result in unstable estimates. This surprising interaction has not been reported in the literature. Previous studies demonstrated that the longer physical or sexual abuse continues the greater the harm done to the child.[18] Finkelhor, however, found no relationship between frequency of abuse and consequences to the child.[19]

The runaway adolescents in this study typically had suffered physical abuse at home, physical abuse on the street, and sexual abuse. They described experiencing abuse at a young age and most had been severely abused. As a consequence, these youths are prematurely on their own trying to function without the skills and resources necessary to become productive members of society. This study has implications for policy makers, health care providers, social service providers, and educators who are trying to meet the needs of these adolescents.

1. Farber, E., Kinast, C., McCoard, W., & Falkner, D. (1984). Violence in families of adolescent runaways. *Child Abuse and Neglect*, 8(3), 295-299.

2. Houghten, T., & Golembiewski, M. (1976). A study of James, J., & Meyerding, J. (1977). Early sexual experience and prostitution. *American Journal of Psychiatry*, 134, 1381-1385.

3. Straus, M., & Gelles, R. (1988). How violent are American families. In G. Hotaling, D. Finkelhor, J. Kirkpatrick, & M. Straus (Eds.), *Family abuse and its consequences: New directors in research*. Beverly Hills, CA: Sage Publications.

4. American Association for Protecting Children. (1986). *Highlights of official child neglect and abuse reporting*, 1984. Denver: American Humane Association.

5. Garbarino, J., & Gilliam, G. (1980). Understanding abusive families. Lexington, MA: Lexington Books.Garbarino, Schellenbach, Sebes, & Associates. (1986). *Troubled youth, troubled families*. New York: Aldine Publishing.

6. Straus, M., & Gelles, R. (1988). How violent are American families. In G. Hotaling, D. Finkelhor, J. Kirkpatrick, & M. Straus (Eds.), *Family abuse and its consequences: New directors in research*. Beverly Hills, CA: Sage Publications.

7. American Association for Protecting Children. (1986). *Highlights of official child neglect and abuse reporting*, 1984. Denver: American Humane Association.

8. Straus, M., & Gelles, R. (1989). *Physical violence in American families*. New Brunswick, NJ: Transaction Publishers.

9. Russell, D.E. (1984). *Sexual exploitation: Rape. Child sexual abuse and workplace harassment*. Newbury Park, CA: Sage Publications, Inc.

10. Finkelhor, D. (1984). *Child sexual abuse: New theories and research*. New York: Free Press.

11. Gomez-Schwartz, B., Horowitz, J.M., & Cardarelli, A.P. (1990). *Child sexual abuse: The initial effects*. Newbury Park, CA: Sage Publications, Inc.

12. Straus, M., & Gelles, R. (1989). *Physical violence in American families*. New Brunswick, NJ: Transaction Publishers.

13. Gomez-Schwartz, B., Horowitz, J.M., & Cardarelli, A.P. (1990). *Child sexual abuse: The initial effects*. Newbury Park, CA: Sage Publications, Inc.

14. Claussen, A.H., & Crittenden, P.M. (1991). Physical and psychological maltreatment: Relations among types of maltreatment. *Child Abuse and Neglect*, 15, 5-18.

15. Adams, G.R., Gullotla, T., & Clancy, M.A. (1985). Homeless adolescents: A descriptive study of similarities and differences between runaways and throwaways. *Adolescence*, 20(79), 715-724.

16. Garbarino, J., Wilson, J., & Garbarino, A. (1986). The adolescent runaway. In J. Garbarino, C. Schellenbach, & J. Sebes (Eds.), *Troubled youth, troubled families*. New York: Aldine.

17. Gomez-Schwartz, B., Horowitz, J.M., & Cardarelli, A.P. (1990). *Child sexual abuse: The initial effects*. Newbury Park, CA: Sage Publications, Inc.

18. Straus, M., & Gelles, R. (1989). *Physical violence in American families*. New Brunswick, NJ: Transaction Publishers.

19. Finkelhor, D. (1979). *Sexually victimized children*. New York: The Free Press.

REFERENCES

Adams, G.R., Gullotla, T., & Clancy, M.A. (1985). Homeless adolescents: A descriptive study of similarities and differences between runaways and throwaways. *Adolescence*, 20(79), 715-724.

American Association for Protecting Children. (1986). *Highlights of official child neglect and abuse reporting, 1984.* Denver: American Humane Association.

American Association for Protecting Children. (1989). *Highlights of official child neglect and abuse reporting, 1987.* Denver: American Humane Association.

Archambault, F.X., & Janus, M.D. (1987). *Physical and sexual abuse: A runaway interview schedule.* Unpublished manuscript, University of Connecticut, Bureau of Educational Research, Storrs.

Archambault, F.X., Welsh, L.A., & Janus, M.D. (1989, April). *Physical abuse of runaways in the home and on the street.* Paper presented at the 1989 annual meeting of the American Educational Research Association, San Francisco, CA.

Archambault, F.X., Welsh, L.A., Janus, M.C., & Brown, S.W. (1990, April). *Some findings on the nature of physical abuse runaways experience on the street.* Paper presented at the 1990 annual meeting of the American Research Association, Boston, MA.

Bagley, C., & Ramsay, R. (1985). *Disrupted childhood and vulnerability to sexual assault: Long-term sequels with implications for counseling.* Paper presented at the Conference on Counselling the Sexual Abuse Survivor, Winnipeg.

Bandura, A. (1986). *Social foundation of thought and action: A social cognitive theory.* Englewood Cliffs, NJ: Prentice Hall.

Briere, J. (1984). *The effects of childhood sexual abuse on later psychological functioning: Defining a "post-sexual-abuse syndrome.* Paper presented at the third national Conference on Sexual Victimization of Children, Washington, DC.

Bryan, J.W., & Freed, F.W. (1982). Corporal punishment: Normative data and sociological and psychological correlates in a community college population. *Journal of Youth and Adolescence*, 11, 77-82.

Byrne, B.M., & Shavelson, R.J. (1986). On the structure of adolescent self-concept. *Journal of Educational Psychology*, 78, 474-481.

Cicchetti, D. (1989). How research on child maltreatment has informed the study of child development: Perspectives from developmental psychology. In D. Cicchetti & V. Carlson (Eds.), *Child maltreatment* (pp. 377-432). New York: Cambridge University Press.

Cicchetti, D., & Carlson, V. (1989). *Child maltreatment: Theory and research on the causes and consequences of child abuse and neglect*. Cambridge, MA: Cambridge University Press.

Claussen, A.H., & Crittenden, P.M. (1991). Physical and psychological maltreatment: Relations among types of maltreatment. *Child Abuse and Neglect*, 15, 5-18.

Conte, J.R. (1984). Progress in treating the sexual abuse of children. -, 258-263.

Courois, C. (1979). The incest experience and its aftermath. Victimology: *An International Journal*, 4, 337-347.

Crittenden, P.M. (1981). Abusing, neglecting, problematic, and adequate dyads: Differentiating by patterns of interaction. *Merrill-Palmer Quarterly*, 27, 201-208.

Culp, R.E., Culp, A.M. (1989). Self-esteem and depression in abusive, neglecting, and nonmaltreating mothers. *Infant Mental Health Journal*, 10(4), 243-251.

Edelbrock, C. (1980). Running away from home: Incidence and correlates among children and youth referred for mental health services. *Journal of Family Issues*, 1(2), 210-228.

Egeland, B., & Sroufe, L.A. (1981). Development sequelae of maltreatment in infancy. *New Directions of Child Development: Developmental Perspectives in Child Maltreatment*, 11, 77-92.

Egeland, B., Sroufe, L.A., & Erickson, M.F. (1983). Developmental consequences of different patterns of maltreatment. *Child Abuse and Neglect*, 7(4), 459-469.

Erickson, M.F., Egeland, B., & Pianta, R. (1989). The effects of maltreatment on the development of young children. In D. Cicchetti & V. Carlson (Eds.), *Child maltreatment: Theory and research on the causes and consequences of child abuse and neglect* (pp. 647-684). New York: Cambridge University Press.

Erikson, E.H. (1968). *Identity: Youth and crisis*. New York: Norton.

Farber, E., & Egeland, B. (1987). Invulnerability among abused and neglected children. In E.J. Anthony & B. Cohler (Eds.), *The invulnerable child* (pp. 253-288). New York: Guiford Press.

Farber, E., & Joseph, J. (1985). The maltreated adolescent: Patterns of physical abuse. *Child Abuse and Neglect*, 9(2), 201-206.

Farber, E., Kinast, C., McCoard, W., & Falkner, D. (1984). Violence in families of adolescent runaways. *Child Abuse and Neglect*, 8(3), 295-299.

Finkelhor, D. (1979). *Sexually victimized children*. New York: The Free Press.

Finkelhor, D. (1984). *Child sexual abuse: New theories and research*. New York: Free Press.

Finkelhor, D. (1986). *A source book on child sexual abuse.* Newbury Park, CA: Sage Publications, Inc.

Finkelhor, D. (1988). *Nursery crimes*. Newbury Park, CA: Sage.

Gabarineo, J., Dubrow, N., Kostelny, K. & Pardo, C. (1992). Children in danger: Coping with the consequences of community violence. San Francisco: Jossey-Bass.

Garbarino, J., & Gilliam, G. (1980). *Understanding abusive families*. Lexington, MA: Lexington Books.

Garbarino, Schellenbach, Sebes, & Associates. (1986). *Troubled youth, troubled families*. New York: Aldine Publishing.

Garbarino, J., Wilson, J., & Garbarino, A. (1986). The adolescent runaway. In J. Garbarino, C. Schellenbach, & J. Sebes (Eds.), *Troubled youth, troubled families*. New York: Aldine Publishing.

Gelles, R.J. (1987). *The violent home*. Newbury Park, CA: Sage Publications, Inc.

Gelles, R.J., & Cornell, C.P. (1990). *Intimate violence in families*. Newbury Park, CA: Sage Publications, Inc.

Goldberg, M. (1972). Runaway Americans. *Mental Hygiene*, 56, 13-21.

Gomez-Schwartz, B., Horowitz, J.M., & Cardarelli, A.P. (1990). *Child sexual abuse: The initial effects*. Newbury Park, CA: Sage Publications, Inc.

Gordon, L., O'Keefe, P. (1985). The "normality" of incest. In A.W. Burgess (Ed.), *Rape and sexual assault* (pp. 70-82). New York: Garland Publishing.

Groth, A.N. (1978). Patterns of sexual assault against children and adolescents. In A.W. Burgess, A.N. Groth, L.L. Homstrom, & S.M. Sgroi (Eds.), *Sexual assault of children and adolescents.* Lexington, MA: Lexington

Hall, G.S. (1904). Adolescence (Vols. I & II). Englewood Cliffs, NJ: Prentice Hall.

Hamburg, D.A. (1986). *Preparing for life: The critical transition of adolescence.* (Annual report of the President). New York: Carnegie Corp.

Hampton, R., & Newberger, E.H. (1988). Child abuse incidence and reporting by hospitals: The significance of severity, class, and race. *American Journal of Public Health,* 75, 56-69.

Hartman, C.R., & Burgess, A.W. (1986). Child sexual abuse: Generic roots of the victim experience. *Journal of Psychotherapy and the Family,* 2(2), 83-92.

Herman, J.A. (1981). *Father-daughter incest.* Cambridge, MA: Harvard University Press.

Herrenkolh, R.C., & Herrenkolh, E.C. (1981). Some antecedents and developmental consequences of child maltreatment. In R. Rizley & D. Cicchetti (Eds.), *Developmental perspectives on child maltreatment.* San Francisco: Jossey-Bass.

Herrenkohl, R.C., Herrenkohl, E.C., Egolf, B., & Seech, M. (1980). The repetition of child abuse: How frequently does it occur? In *The abused child in the family and in the community*: Selected papers from the second International Congress on Child Abuse and Neglect, London, 1978, Vol. 1, edited by C.H. Kempe, A.W. Franklin, & C. Cooper. Oxford: Pergamon Press.

Hill, J.P. & Holbeck, G.N. (1986). Attachment and autonomy during adolescence. In I.G. Whitehurst (Ed.), *Annals of child development*: Vol. I (pp. 145-189). Greenwich, CT: JAI.

Houghten, T., & Golembiewski, M. (1976). A study of James, J., & Meyerding, J. (1977). Early sexual experience and prostitution. *American Journal of Psychiatry,* 134, 1381-1385.

House Committee on Education and Labor, Subcomittee of Human Resources. (1984). *Juvenile Justice, Runaway Youth and Missing Children's Act*, Amendments, 98th congress, 2nd Session, 7 March.

Janus, M., Archambault, F.X., & Welsh, L.A. (1988). *Physical and sexual abuse in runaway homeless youth.* Paper presented at the 96th annual meeting of the American Psychological Association, Atlanta, GA.

Janus, M.D., McCormack, A., Burgess, A.W., & Hartman, C. (1987). *Adolescent runaways: Causes and consequences.* Lexington, MA: Lexington Books.

Jenkins, R.L., & Boyer, A. (1968). Types of delinquent behavior and background factors. *International Journal of Social Psychiatry,* 14, 65-75.

Joreskog, K., & Sorbom, D. (1986). *LISREL: Analysis of linear structural relationships by the method of maximum likelihood.* Morresville, IN: Scientific Software.

Kaplan, H.B. (1978). Social class, self-derogation and deviant response. *Social Psychiatry,* 13, 19-28.

Kercher, G., & McShane, M. (1983). *The prevalence of child sexual abuse victimization in an adult sample of Texas residents.* Huntsville, TX: Sam Houston State University.

Liebertoff, K. (1980). The runaway child in America. *Journal of Family Issues,* 1, 151-164.

Lynch, M.A., & Roberts, J. (1977). Predicting child abuse: Signs of bonding failure in the maternity hospital. *British Medical Journal,* 1, 624-626.

Martin, H.P. (1980). The consequences of being abused and neglected: How the child fares. In C.H. Kempe & R.E. Helfer (Eds.), *The battered child* (3rd ed.). Chicago: University of Chicago Press.

McCormack, A., Janus, M.D., & Burgess, A.W. (1986). Runaway youths and sexual victimization: Gender differences in an adolescent runaway population. *Child Abuse and Neglect,* 10, 387-395.

Meiselman, K. (1979). *Incest: A psychiatric study of causes and effects with treatment recommendations.* San Francisco: Jossey-Bass.

Muus, R.E. (1990). Adolescent behavior and society. New York: McGraw-Hill Publishing Co.

National Center on Child Abuse and Neglect (NCCAN). (1981). *Study findings: National study of incidence and severity of child abuse and neglect.* Washington, DC: Department of Health, Education, and Welfare.

Oates, K. (1986). *Child abuse and neglect: What happens eventually?* New York: Brunner/Mazel.

Olsen, L., & Holmes, W. (1983). *Youth at risk: Adolescents and maltreatment.* Boston, MA: Center for Applied Social Research.

Opinion Research Corporation. (1976). *National statistical survey of runaway youth.* Princeton, NJ.

Peters, S.D. (1984). *The relationship between childhood sexual victimization and adult depression among Afro-American and White women.* Unpublished doctoral dissertation, University of California, Los Angeles.

Piaget, J. (1952). *The origins of intelligence in children.* New York: International Press.

Pianta, R., Egeland, B., & Erickson, M.E. (1989). The antecedents of maltreatment: Results of the mother-child interaction research project. In D. Cicchetti & V. Carlson (Eds.), *Child maltreatment: Theory and research on the causes and consequences of child abuse and neglect* (pp. 203-253). New York: Cambridge University Press.

Powers, J., & Eckenrode, J. (1988). The maltreatment of adolescents. *Child Abuse and Neglect,* 12(2), 189-200.

Reich, J.W., & Gutierre, S.E. (1979). Escape/aggression incidence in sexually abused juvenile delinquents. *Criminal Justice and Behavior,* 6, 239-243.

Reidy, T.J. (1977). The aggressive characteristics of abused and neglected children. *Journal of Clinical Psychology,* 33, 1140-1145.

Rosenberg, M. (1965). *Society and adolescent self-image.* Princeton, NJ: Princeton University Press.

Rosenberg, M. (1989). *Society and the adolescent self-image.* Middletown, CT: Wesleyan University Press.

Rosenberg, M., & Simmons, R.G. (1972). Black and white self-esteem: *The urban school child.* Washington, DC: American Sociological Association.

Russell, D.E. (1984). *Sexual exploitation: Rape. Child sexual abuse and workplace harassment.* Newbury Park, CA: Sage Publications, Inc.

Russell, D.E. (1986). *The secret trauma: Incest in the lives of girls and women.* New York: Basic Books.

Schneider-Rosen, K, & Cicchetti, D. (1984). The relationship between affect and cognition in maltreated infants: Quality of attachment and the development of visual self-recognition. *Child Development,* 55, 648-658.

Sedney, M.A., & Brooks, B. (1984). Factors associated with a history of childhood sexual experience in a nonclinical female population. *Journal of American Academy of Child Psychiatry*, 23, 215-218.

Sibler, E., & Tippett, J.S. (1965). Self-esteem: Clinical assessment and measurement validation. *Psychological Reports*, 16, 1017-1071.

Silbert, M.H., & Pines, A.M. (1981). Sexual child abuse as an antecedent to prostitution. *Child Abuse and Neglect*, 5, 407-411.

Song, I.S., & Hattie, J. (1984). Home environment, self-concept, and academic achievement: A causal modeling approach. *Journal of Educational Psychology*, 76(6), 1269-1281.

Steele, B.F., & Pollock, C.B. (1974). Psychiatric study of abusive parents. In R.E. Helfer & C.H. Kempe (Eds.), *The battered child*. Chicago: University of Chicago Press.

Steinberg, L. (1987). The impact of puberty on family relations: Effects of pubertal status and pubertal timing. *Developmental Psychology*, 23, 451-460.

Straus, M.A. (1979). Measuring intrafamily conflict and violence: The conflict tactics (CT) scales. *Journal of Marriage and the Family*, 4(1), 75-87.

Straus, M., & Gelles, R. (1986). Societal change and change in family violence from 1975-1985 as revealed by two national surveys. *Journal of Marriage and the Family*, 48, 465-489.

Straus, M., & Gelles, R. (1988). How violent are American families. In G. Hotaling, D. Finkelhor, J. Kirkpatrick, & M. Straus (Eds.), *Family abuse and its consequences: New directors in research*. Beverly Hills, CA: Sage Publications.

Straus, M., & Gelles, R. (1989). *Physical violence in American families*. New Brunswick, NJ: Transaction Publishers.

Straus, M., Gelles, R., & Steinmetz, S. (1981). *Behind closed doors: Violence in the American family*. Newbury Park, CA: Sage Publications Inc.

Summit, R. (1983). The child abuse accommodation syndrome. Child Abuse and Neglect: *The International Journal*, 7(2), 177-193.

Tabachnick, B.G., & Fidell, L.S. (1989). *Using multivariate statistics*. New York: Harper Collins.

Tufts New England Medical Center Study. (1984). Final report to the Department of Juvenile Justice and Delinquency Prevention.

(Sexual Abuse Treatment Project at Tufts.) Boston, MA: New England Medical Center.

Walker, L.S., & Green, J.W. (1986). The social context of adolescent self-esteem. *Journal of Youth and Adolescence*, 15(4), 315-322.

Wylie, R.C. (1989). *Measures of self-concept*. Lincoln: University of Nebraska Press.

Index

Please remember that this is a library book,
and that it belongs only temporarily to each
person who uses it. Be considerate. Do
not write in this, or any, library book.

DATE DUE

OC 22 '03			
OC 15 '06			
5/26/08			
GAYLORD			PRINTED IN U.S.A.